U0084453

序 言

　　爲了因應即將施測的國中教育會考,「學習出版公司」於去年率先出版「國中會考英語聽力測驗 ①」,其內容根據教育部公布的聽力題型編撰,已有眾多公私立國中採用,反應熱烈,效果良好。由於許多老師的詢問與要求,希望能有更多符合國中教育會考英文聽力的練習,「國中會考英語聽力測驗 ②」因應而生。

　　「國中會考英語聽力測驗 ②」仿照「國中會考英語聽力測驗 ①」製作方式,共十二回,每回有三十題。比照「103 年國中教育會考英語聽力測驗」公布試題的範例,國中常用1200字,分成三部分:辨識句意、基本問答、言談理解,題目皆是生活常用情景及對話,唯一不同的是,爲了讓同學有較多的練習,本書每份題組比公布的試題多了十題,是讓同學可以做好最完善的準備。

　　聽力訓練別無他法,就是練習、練習,再練習,便熟能生巧(Practice makes perfect.)。本書題目十二回,共 360 題,提供莘莘學子練習最新題型的機會。每題都有詳細的説明和註釋,解除所有的疑問。

　　本書編寫活潑生動,符合生活美語,有些美國人的習慣口語,特別在「背景説明」中詳加解釋,一般中國人不會的慣用語,就是勝過別人的關鍵。在編審及校對的每一階段,均力求完善,但恐有疏漏之處,誠盼各界先進不吝批評指正。

編者 謹識

國中教育會考英語科聽力測驗說明

一、考試內容

教育會考英語科命題以《國民中小學九年一貫課程綱要》分段能力指標為依據。考試內容如下：

（一）**主題與體裁**：符合趣味化、實用化、多元化及生活化的原則，呼應十項基本能力的精神。

（二）**溝通功能**：包括日常交談、社交應對、教室用語等一般人際溝通之語言能力。依其功能可分為問候、感謝、道歉、同意、請求、問路、打電話等類別。

（三）**語言成分**：

1. 字彙：詳見課程綱要附錄四基本之1200個字彙。
2. 語法結構：詳見課程綱要附錄五之基本語言結構參考表。

二、說明

教育會考英語科的聽力及閱讀測驗內容皆為基本、核心、重要的概念，試題編寫嘗試多種體裁及主題，且其語言使用重視整體自然情境，而非繁瑣、片斷的記憶。

三、聽力測驗

103年教育會考英語科聽力測驗說明如下：

（一）**評量理由**：

「聽力」是學習任何語言的基礎能力（包括閩南語、客語……等），國民中小學九年一貫課程綱要亦明訂英語科課程同時注重聽、說、讀、寫的教學，因此若只評量學生閱讀能力，考試結果僅能有限說明學生的局部英語能力。

教育會考配合英語科課程綱要內涵，納入英語聽力測驗，針對國中生進行英語閱讀與聽力綜合評量，將能更有效的評量國中畢業生真正的英語能力。

（二）聽力及閱讀複合題本：

教育會考英語科聽力測驗與英語閱讀測驗合併實施，考試時間共80分鐘，前 15～20 分鐘先進行聽力測驗，**待所有聽力試題播音完畢後，考生即可直接繼續作答閱讀測驗，不須等待監考老師指示。**

聽力與閱讀測驗合計共 60～75 題，其中前 20～30 題爲聽力試題，後 40～45 題爲閱讀試題，試題本合併爲一，**題號連續，共用一張答案卡。**

聽力試題包含語音檔與試題本內的文字。題型均爲 3 選 1 的單選題，分爲辨識句意（3～10 題，單句+圖表）、基本問答（7～10 題，簡易對話）及言談理解（10～15 題，短文及對話，評量細節、推論、猜字、主旨等）3 部分。以下爲聽力及閱讀測驗複合題本架構：

	題型	測驗內容（評量目標）	題數分配
聽力 （20-30 題） （三選一）	單題	辨識句意（單句+圖表）	3-10
		基本問答（單一對話）	7-10
		言談理解 （短文及對話，評量細節、推論、猜字、主旨等）	10
聽力測驗每題均播音兩次，兩次播音之間停頓 5 秒。			
閱讀 （40-45 題） （四選一）	單題	語言基礎成分 （字彙/語意+語法）	12-20
	題組	篇章理解 （克漏字+整段式）	25-35
聽力 + 閱讀：60-75 題			

（三）聽力測驗之作答說明：

正式測驗時，每道試題播音兩次，兩次播音之間停頓約 5 秒。每一部分正式播放考生要作答的試題之前，均會先播放作答說明。聽力測驗內容共分爲 3 部分，以下爲各部分之作答說明。

【英語科＜聽力等級＞】

◎精 熟：能聽懂主題熟悉、訊息稍為複雜、段落較長的言談，指出言
　　　　　談的主旨與結論等重要訊息，並從言談中言語及其他如語調
　　　　　與節奏等線索做出推論；能理解短片及廣播節目的大意。

◎基 礎：能聽懂日常生活主題、訊息單純的短篇言談，指出言談的主
　　　　　旨與結論等重要訊息，並從言談中明顯的言語及其他如語調
　　　　　與節奏等線索做出簡易推論。

◎待加強：僅能聽懂單句及簡易問答；僅能有限的理解短篇言談。

第一部分：

（以下是你會聽到的語音播放內容，不會顯示在題本中）

聽力測驗 第一部分：辨識句意 作答說明：第 1 題到第 3 題，每
題有 3 張圖片，請依據所聽到的單句，選出符合描述的圖片。每題
播放兩次。請看示例題。你會看到 A、B、C 三個選項。

（以下是你在題本中會看到的選項）

(A) 　　　(B) 　　　(C)

（以下是你會聽到的語音播放內容，不會顯示在題本中）

然後，你會聽到

Mary is wearing a dress and glasses.

　　　（停頓約 5 秒）

Mary is wearing a dress and glasses.

　　　（停頓約 5 秒）

依據所播放的內容，正確答案應該選 A，請將答案卡該題 A 的地方
塗黑、塗滿。

　　　（停頓數秒）

現在開始播放試題。

第二部分：

（以下是你會聽到的語音播放內容，不會顯示在題本中）

聽力測驗 第二部分：基本問答 作答說明：第4題到第10題每題均有3個選項，請依據所聽到的對話問句，選出一個最適合的回答。每題播放兩次。請看示例題。你會看到 A、B、C 三個選項。

（以下是你在題本中會看到的選項，不會在語音播放時念出聲音）

(A) She is talking to the teacher.
(B) She is a student in my class.
(C) She is wearing a beautiful dress.

（以下是你會聽到的語音播放內容，不會顯示在題本中）

然後，你會聽到

Who's the girl over there?

（停頓約5秒）

Who's the girl over there?

（停頓約5秒）

依據所播放的內容，正確答案應該選B，請將答案卡該題B的地方塗黑、塗滿。

（停頓數秒）

現在開始播放試題。

第三部分：

（以下是你會聽到的語音播放內容，不會顯示在題本中）

聽力測驗　第三部分：言談理解　作答說明：第 11 題到第 20 題每題均有三個選項，請依據所聽到的對話或短文內容，選出一個最適合的答案。每題播放兩次。請看示例題。你會看到 A、B、C 三個選項。

（以下是你在題本中會看到的選項，不會在語音播放時念出聲音）

(A) 9:50. (B) 10:00. (C) 10:10.

（以下是你會聽到的語音播放內容，不會顯示在題本中）

然後，你會聽到

（男聲）Cathy! It's almost time to go to bed.

（小女孩聲）But it's only nine-fifty. I still have ten more minutes to play. Right?

（男聲）Right! But only ten more minutes.

Question: What time should Cathy go to bed?

（停頓約 5 秒）

（男聲）Cathy! It's almost time to go to bed.

（小女孩聲）But it's only nine-fifty. I still have ten more minutes to play. Right?

（男聲）Right! But only ten more minutes.

Question: What time should Cathy go to bed?

（停頓約 5 秒）

依據所播放的內容，正確答案應該選 B，請將答案卡該題 B 的地方塗黑、塗滿。

（停頓數秒）

現在開始播放試題。

　　所有聽力試題播音結束後，**請考生直接繼續作答閱讀測驗，不須等**待監考老師的指示。

TEST 1

第一部分：辨識句意（第 1-10 題，共 10 題）

作答說明：　第 1-10 題每題均有三個選項，請依據所聽到的單句，選出符合描述的圖片。

示例題：你會看到

(A)   (B)   (C)

依據所播放的内容，正確答案應該選 A，請將答案紙該題「Ⓐ」的地方塗黑、塗滿，即 ●Ⓑ©。

---

1. (A)   (B)   (C)

2. (A)   (B)   (C)

8. (A)　　　(B)　　　(C)

9. (A)　　　(B)　　　(C)

10. (A)　　　(B)　　　(C)

第二部分：基本問答（第 11-20 題，共 10 題）

作答說明：　第 11-20 題每題均有三個選項，請依據所聽到的對話問句，選出一個最適合的回答。

> 示例題：你會看到
>
> (A) She is talking to the teacher.
> (B) She is a student in my class.
> (C) She is wearing a beautiful dress.
>
> 依據所播放的內容，正確答案應該選 B，請將答案紙該題「⑧」的地方塗黑、塗滿，即 Ⓐ ● Ⓒ。

11. (A) She's five-foot-five.

(B) She's twelve years old.

(C) She's in school now.

12. (A) Sorry, he's not home.

(B) Thanks. How thoughtful of you.

(C) Maybe next time.

13. (A) He'll be fine. It's probably just a cold.

(B) He'll be on time. You're probably just getting old.

(C) He'll be in line. They probably need to be told.

14. (A) You're welcome.

(B) Don't mention it.

(C) The pleasure is all mine.

15. (A) Calm down. It's not that urgent.

(B) Oh, knock it off. It's not that hot.

(C) Relax. They wouldn't forget about us.

16. (A) Summer is my favorite time of year.

(B) I'm thinking about a trip to Spain.

(C) Meet me at the corner.

17. (A) That was Mary on the phone.

(B) Ring the bell if you know the answer.

(C) She said, "Please turn off your cell phones."

18. (A) Joe is the most talented.
    (B) Let's play ball.
    (C) They have no class.

19. (A) I had time.
    (B) I got lost.
    (C) I took the bus.

20. (A) They have free wireless Internet access.
    (B) No, thanks. I'm good.
    (C) Several new shops have opened in the area.

第三部分：言談理解（第 21-30 題，共 10 題）

作答說明： 第 21-30 題每題均有三個選項，請依據所聽到的對話或短文內容，選出一個最適合的答案。

示例題：你會看到

(A) 9:50.　　(B) 10:00.　　(C) 10:10.

依據所播放的內容，正確答案應該選 B，請將答案紙該題「Ⓑ」的地方塗黑、塗滿，即Ⓐ●Ⓒ。

---

21. (A) In a bank.
    (B) In an airport.
    (C) In a supermarket.

22. (A) Watching television.
    (B) Paying a bill.
    (C) Getting dressed.

23. (A) 11:00 p.m.
    (B) 12:00 a.m.
    (C) 11:00 a.m.

24. (A) In a hotel room.
    (B) In a bakery.
    (C) In a clothing store.

25. (A) Leave a message for
        Kevin Reynolds.
    (B) Speak with Kevin
        Reynolds.
    (C) Schedule a meeting
        with Kevin Reynolds.

26. (A) A cup of green tea.
    (B) A cup of green tea
        with cream.
    (C) A cup of green tea
        with sugar.

27. (A) Call a plumber.
    (B) Drive her car.
    (C) Look for the keys.

28. (A) Brother–sister.
    (B) Uncle–niece.
    (C) Father–daughter.

29. (A) A man was shot and
        killed.
    (B) A cat got stuck in a
        tree.
    (C) A house caught on
        fire.

30. (A) Chinese restaurant.
    (B) Italian restaurant.
    (C) Fast-food restaurant.

TEST 1 詳解

第一部分：辨識句意

1. (**A**) (A)   (B)   (C)

Jane is holding an umbrella. 珍正拿著一把雨傘。

* hold〔hold〕v. 拿著；握著   umbrella〔ʌm'brɛlə〕n. 雨傘

2. (**A**) (A)   (B)   (C)

The cat has killed a mouse. 貓殺死了一隻老鼠。

* mouse〔maʊs〕n. 老鼠

3. (**B**) (A)   (B)   (C)

A bird has landed on the flower. 有隻鳥降落在花朵上。

* land〔lænd〕v. 降落   flower〔'flaʊɚ〕n. 花

4. (**C**) (A)  (B)  (C)

Molly is holding a gun. 莫莉握著一支手槍。

* gun〔gʌn〕*n.* 手槍

5. (**B**) (A)  (B) (C)

Jimmy is ice-skating. 吉米在溜冰。

* ice-skate〔'aɪs,sket〕*v.* 溜冰

6. (**C**) (A)  (B)  (C)

Lucy will enjoy a bowl of soup.

露西將要享用一碗湯。

* enjoy〔ɪn'dʒɔɪ〕*v.* 享用；享受

  bowl〔bol〕*n.* 碗；一碗的量　　soup〔sup〕*n.* 湯

7. (**B**) (A) 　　(B) 　　(C)

Sarah is doing her homework.

莎拉在做功課。

* homework〔'hom,wɜk〕*n.* 功課；回家作業

8. (**A**) (A) 　　(B) 　　(C)

It's a very windy day. 這是個風很大的日子。

* windy〔'wɪndɪ〕*adj.* 颳風的；多風的

9. (**A**) (A) 　　(B) 　　(C)

Jimmy is on the swing. 吉米在鞦韆上。

* swing〔swɪŋ〕*n.* 鞦韆

10. (**B**) (A)  (B)  (C)

Kim has long, straight hair.

金有著又長又直的頭髮。

* straight〔stret〕*adj.* 直的

第二部分：基本問答

11. (**B**) Your daughter is so tall! How old is she?

你的女兒好高！她幾歲？

(A) She's five-foot-five. 她五呎五吋高。

(B) She's twelve years old. 她十二歲。

(C) She's in school now. 她現在在學校。

* foot〔fut〕*n.* 呎；英尺【一英尺為 30.48 公分】
  five-foot-five 五呎五吋高（ = *five feet and five inches tall* ）

12. (**B**) Congratulations! I bought a gift for you.

恭喜！我買了一個禮物給你。

(A) Sorry, he's not home. 抱歉，他不在家。

(B) Thanks. How thoughtful of you.

謝謝。你真體貼。

(C) Maybe next time. 或許下一次。

* congratulations〔kən͵grætʃəˈleʃənz〕*n. pl.* (感嘆詞) 恭喜！
  gift〔gɪft〕*n.* 禮物
  thoughtful〔ˈθɔtfəl〕*adj.* 體貼的   maybe〔ˈmebɪ〕*adv.* 或許
  next time 下一次

13. (**A**) John went to the doctor today. I hope it's nothing
serious. 約翰今天去看醫生。我希望不是什麼嚴重的事情。

(A) He'll be fine. It's probably just a cold.
他不會有事的。可能只是感冒。

(B) He'll be on time. You're probably just getting old.
他會準時到達。你可能只是變老了。

(C) He'll be in line. They probably need to be told.
他會有希望。他們可能需要被告知。

* ***go to the doctor*** 去看醫生　　hope〔hop〕*v.* 希望
serious〔'sɪrɪes〕*adj.* 嚴重的
fine〔faɪn〕*adj.* 很健康的；精神好的
probably〔'prɑbəblɪ〕*adv.* 可能　　cold〔kold〕*n.* 感冒
on time 準時
be in line 等待；有希望 <*for*>【詳見背景說明】

14. (**C**) It's a pleasure to meet you. Becky has told us so much
about you.
很高興認識你。貝琪已經告訴我們很多關於你的事。

(A) You're welcome. 不客氣。

(B) Don't mention it. 不客氣。

(C) The pleasure is all mine. 這是我的榮幸。

* pleasure〔'plɛʒɚ〕*n.* 快樂的事；榮幸
meet〔mit〕*v.* 認識；遇見　　***You're welcome.*** 不客氣。
mention〔'mɛnʃən〕*v.* 提到
Don't mention it. 不用謝；不客氣。
The pleasure is all mine. 這是我的榮幸。

15. (**B**) Aren't you dying out here? It must be two thousand
degrees in the shade!
你在外面不會死掉嗎？那樹蔭下想必有兩千度吧！

(A) Calm down. It's not that urgent.

冷靜下來。沒那麼緊急。

(B) Oh, knock it off. It's not that hot.

喔，別吵了。沒那麼熱。

(C) Relax. They wouldn't forget about us.

請放鬆。他們不會忘了我們。

* *out here* 在外面 (= *outside*)
degree〔dɪ'gri〕 *n.* (氣溫) 度　　shade〔ʃed〕 *n.* 陰暗處；樹蔭
in the shade 在陰暗處；在樹蔭下　　*calm down* 冷靜下來
urgent〔'ɝdʒənt〕 *adj.* 迫切的；緊急的
knock it off 住口；別吵　　relax〔rɪ'læks〕 *v.* 放鬆
forget〔fə'gɛt〕 *v.* 忘記

16. (**B**) Summer is just around the corner. Got any plans?

夏天要來臨了。有什麼計畫嗎？

(A) Summer is my favorite time of year.

夏天是我一年中最喜愛的時光。

(B) I'm thinking about a trip to Spain.

我在考慮去西班牙旅行。

(C) Meet me at the corner. 在那角落跟我會面。

* corner〔'kɔrnə〕 *n.* 角落　　just〔dʒʌst〕 *adv.* 正要
Got any plans? 有什麼計畫嗎？ (= *Have you got any plans?*)
be around the corner 即將到來　　plan〔plæn〕 *n.* 計畫
favorite〔'fevərɪt〕 *adj.* 最喜愛的　　*think about* 考慮
trip〔trɪp〕 *n.* 旅行　　Spain〔spen〕 *n.* 西班牙【歐洲西南部】

17. (**C**) Did you hear what she said? My cell phone was
ringing. 你有聽到她說什麼嗎？我的手機那時正在響。

(A) That was Mary on the phone. 電話上的是瑪麗。

(B) Ring the bell if you know the answer.

如果你知道答案，請按鈴。

(C) She said, "Please turn off your cell phones."

她說：「請關掉你們的手機。」

* *cell phone* 手機　　ring〔rɪŋ〕v. 鈴響

on the phone 講電話　　bell〔bɛl〕n. 鈴；鈴聲

ring the bell 響鈴；敲鈴　　*turn off* 關掉（電源）

18. (**A**) Who is the best athlete in my class?

誰是我班上最優秀的運動員？

(A) Joe is the most talented. 喬是最有天賦的。

(B) Let's play ball. 一起打球吧。

(C) They have no class. 他們沒課。

* athlete〔'æθlɪt〕n. 運動員

class〔klæs〕n. 班級；上課（時間）

talented〔'tæləntɪd〕adj. 有天賦的；有才能的

let's + *V*. 讓我們一起～吧

19. (**C**) How did you get here? By taxi or bus?

你怎麼到這裡的？搭計程車還是巴士？

(A) I had time. 我有時間。

(B) I got lost. 我迷路了。

(C) I took the bus. 我搭巴士。

* get〔gɛt〕v. 到達　　*by* + 交通工具　搭～

get lost 迷路　　take〔tek〕v. 搭乘

20. (**B**) I'm going to the coffee shop. Can I get you anything?

我要去咖啡店。我能幫你買什麼嗎？

(A) They have free wireless Internet access.

他們有免費的無線上網。

(B) No, thanks. I'm good. 不，謝謝。我很飽。

(C) Several new shops have opened in the area.

這地區有好幾家新開的店。

* shop〔ʃɑp〕*n.* 商店　　get〔gɛt〕*v.* 買
free〔fri〕*adj.* 免費的　　wireless〔'waɪrlɪs〕*adj.* 無線的
Internet〔'ɪntɚ,nɛt〕*n.* 網際網路
access〔'æksɛs〕*n.* 接近或使用的權利
Internet access 上網　　***I'm good.*** 我很飽。(= *I am full.*)
open〔'opən〕*v.* 張開；開業　　area〔'ɛrɪə〕*n.* 地方；地區

第三部分：言談理解

21.(**B**) W : Would you prefer an aisle or window seat?

女：你比較喜歡靠走道還是靠窗的座位？

M : Aisle seat, please.

男：請給我靠走道的座位。

W : OK, you're all set. Please present your boarding

pass at Gate 3.

女：好的，爲你準備好了。請在三號登機門出示你的登機證。

Question：Where are the speakers? 說話者在哪裡？

(A) In a bank. 在銀行。

(B) In an airport. 在機場。

(C) In a supermarket. 在超級市場。

* prefer〔prɪ'fɝ〕*v.* 比較喜歡　　aisle〔aɪl〕*n.* 走道
seat〔sit〕*n.* 座位　　***be all set*** 準備就緒的 (= *be ready*)
present〔prɪ'zɛnt〕*v.* 出示
board〔bord〕*v.* 上 (飛機、火車等)
boarding pass 登機證
gate〔get〕*n.* 大門；出入口【在此指「登機門」(boading gate) 】
bank〔bæŋk〕*n.* 銀行　　airport〔'ɛr,port〕*n.* 機場
supermarket〔'supɚ,mɑrkɪt〕*n.* 超級市場

22. (**A**) M：Would you hand me the television remote?

男：妳可以把電視遙控器拿給我嗎？

W：I would if I knew where it was.

女：如果我知道在哪，我會拿給你。

M：It's on the dresser, next to my wallet.

男：就在梳妝台上，我皮夾旁邊。

Question：What is the man doing? 男士正在做什麼？

(A) Watching television. 看電視。

(B) Paying a bill. 付帳單。

(C) Getting dressed. 穿衣服。

* hand〔hænd〕*v.* 拿給
remote〔rɪ'mot〕*n.* 遙控器 (= *remote control*)
dresser〔'drɛsɚ〕*n.* 梳妝台　　***next to*** 在～旁邊
wallet〔'wɑlɪt〕*n.* 皮夾　　bill〔bɪl〕*n.* 帳單
dress〔drɛs〕*v.* 給…穿衣服
get dressed 穿衣服 (= *put on clothes*)

23. (**A**) W：Excuse me, sir. When does the next train leave for Fresno?

女：先生，不好意思。下一班去弗雷斯諾的火車是幾點？

M：Sorry, lady. Not until five o'clock tomorrow morning.

男：小姐，很抱歉。要到明天早上五點才有。

W：Oh, no! What am I going to do for the next six hours?

女：喔，不！那我接下來的六個小時要做什麼？

Question：What time is it now? 現在幾點？

(A) 11:00 p.m. 晚上十一點。

(B) 12:00 a.m. 半夜十二點。

(C) 11:00 a.m. 上午十一點。

* **Excuse me**. 對不起。【用於引起對方注意】
  leave for 出發;前往
  Fresno ('frɛzno) *n*. 弗雷斯諾【美國加州中部的城市】
  not until… 直到…才~　　**a.m.** 上午 (= *ante meridiem*)
  p.m. 下午 (= *post meridiem*)

24. (**A**) M : Let's go grab a drink down in the lobby. The lounge
            should still be open.

    男:我們一起去大廳買個飲料喝。休息室應該還開著。

    W : I'd rather not. It's getting late and we've got an
         early flight to catch.

    女:我寧可不要。時間很晚了,而且我們得趕上早班的飛機。

    M : Well, I'm going. Don't wait up for me then.

    男:嗯,那我走了。那麼先睡覺別等我了。

    Question : Where are the speakers?

    　　　　　　說話者在哪裡?

    (A) In a hotel room. 在飯店房間裡。

    (B) In a bakery. 在麵包店。

    (C) In a clothing store. 在服飾店。

* **go + V**. 去~ (= *go to V*. = *go and V*.)
  grab〔græb〕*v*. 抓;趕緊 (吃東西或睡覺等)
  drink〔drɪŋk〕*n*. 飲料　　lobby〔'labɪ〕*n*. 大廳
  lounge〔laʊndʒ〕*n*. 休息室;會客廳
  would rather + **V**. 寧可~;寧願~
  flight〔flaɪt〕*n*. 班機
  catch〔kætʃ〕*v*. 趕上　　**wait up for** 等待…而不睡
  hotel〔ho'tɛl〕*n*. 飯店;旅館
  bakery〔'bekərɪ〕*n*. 麵包店
  clothing〔'kloðɪŋ〕*n*.【集合名詞】衣服

25. (**B**)　W : Yes, I'm calling for Kevin Reynolds.

　　女：是的，我打來找凱文・雷恩萊諾。

　　M : Mr. Reynolds is in a meeting.　Would you like his
　　　　voice mail?

　　男：雷恩萊諾先生現在在開會。妳要在他的語音信箱留言嗎？

　　W : No.　I'll try him later this afternoon.

　　女：不。我今天下午晚點會再找他。

　　Question : What does the woman want to do?

　　　　　　　這位女士想要做什麼？

　　(A) Leave a message for Kevin Reynolds.

　　　　留言給凱文・雷恩萊諾。

　　(B) Speak with Kevin Reynolds.　和凱文・雷恩萊諾講話。

　　(C) Schedule a meeting with Kevin Reynolds.

　　　　和凱文・雷恩萊諾安排會議時間。

　　* meeting〔'mitɪŋ〕*n.* 會議　　***voice mail*** 語音信箱
　　　try〔traɪ〕*v.* 找（某人）商談；問看看（某人）
　　　try him later 晚點找他；晚點打電話給他（= *call him later*）
　　　message〔'mɛsɪdʒ〕*n.* 訊息；留言
　　　leave a message 留言
　　　schedule〔'skɛdʒul〕*v.* 安排…的時間

26. (**A**)　M : Do you have green tea?　I'll have a cup of that if
　　　　you do.

　　男：你們有綠茶嗎？如果有的話，我要一杯。

　　W : Yes, we do.　Would you care for any cream or sugar?

　　女：是的，我們有。那你想要加奶精還是糖？

　　M : No, thanks.　I take it without.

　　男：不，謝謝。我什麼都不加。

　　Question : What does the man want?　男士要什麼？

(A) A cup of green tea. 一杯綠茶。

(B) A cup of green tea with cream. 一杯有奶精的綠茶。

(C) A cup of green tea with sugar. 一杯有加糖的綠茶。

* **_green tea_** 綠茶　　**_care for_** 喜歡；想要

　　cream〔krim〕_n._ 奶油；奶精　　sugar〔'ʃugə〕_n._ 糖

　　take〔tek〕_v._ 吃；喝（= _drink_）

　　without〔wɪ'ðaʊt〕_adv._ 在沒有…的情況下【詳見背景説明】

27. (**C**) W : Did you move my car keys?

　　女：你有動過我的車鑰匙嗎？

　　M : Of course not. Why would I do that?

　　男：當然沒有。我為什麼要那麼做？

　　W : I don't know. They were here a minute ago.

　　女：我不知道。鑰匙一分鐘前還在這裡。

　　Question : What will the woman most likely do next?

　　　　　　女士接下來最可能做什麼？

　　(A) Call a plumber. 打電話給水管工人。

　　(B) Drive her car. 開她的車。

　　(C) Look for the keys. 找鑰匙。

　　* move〔muv〕_v._ 移動　　key〔ki〕_n._ 鑰匙

　　of course 當然　　likely〔'laɪklɪ〕_adv._ 可能

　　next〔nɛkst〕_adv._ 接下來　　plumber〔'plʌmə〕_n._ 水管工人

　　look for 尋找

28. (**C**) M : Hey, Sarah, would you hold off on piano practice

　　　　　　for a few minutes?

　　男：嘿，莎拉，妳可以暫停練習鋼琴幾分鐘嗎？

　　W : Why, Dad?

　　女：為什麼，爸爸？

M : I'm on the phone with your uncle Jack.

男： 我在跟妳的叔叔傑克講電話。

Question : What is the relationship between the speakers?

說話者的關係是什麼？

(A) Brother–sister. 兄妹。

(B) Uncle–niece. 叔姪。

(C) Father–daughter. 父女。

* ***hold off on*** 延遲；拖延 (= *delay*)
  piano〔pɪˈæno〕*n.* 鋼琴　　practice〔ˈpræktɪs〕*n.* 練習
  uncle〔ˈʌŋkl̩〕*n.* 叔叔；舅舅　　***on the phone*** 講電話
  relationship〔rɪˈleʃənˌʃɪp〕*n.* 關係
  niece〔nis〕*n.* 姪女；外甥女　　daughter〔ˈdɔtɚ〕*n.* 女兒

29. (**C**) W : Did you hear all the sirens this morning?

女：你今天早上有聽到警報聲嗎？

M : Yes. There was a house fire over on Lincoln Avenue.

男：有。在林肯大道有房子起火。

W : I hope no one was injured.

女：我希望沒人受傷。

Question : What happened this morning?

今天早上發生了什麼事？

(A) A man was shot and killed.

有一名男子被射殺身亡。

(B) A cat got stuck in a tree.

有一隻貓困在樹上。

(C) A house caught on fire.

有間房子起火。

* siren (ˈsaɪrən) *n.* 警報器　　fire (faɪr) *n.* 火災；火警

Lincoln (ˈlɪŋkən) *n.* 林肯【美國第十六任總統】

happen (ˈhæpən) *v.* 發生

avenue (ˈævəˌnju) *n.* 大道　　injure (ˈɪndʒɚ) *v.* 使受傷

shoot (ʃut) *v.* 射殺【三態為：shoot-shot-shot】

kill (kɪl) *v.* 殺死　　　stuck (stʌk) *adj.* 卡住無法動彈的

catch on fire 著火 (= *catch fire*)

30. (**C**)　M：Are you ready to order?

男：妳準備好點餐了嗎？

W：Yes, I'll have two cheeseburgers and a large Coke.

女：是的，我要兩個起司漢堡和一杯大杯可口可樂。

M：Is that for here or to go?

男：要內用還是外帶？

Question：What kind of restaurant is it?

這是哪種餐廳？

(A) Chinese restaurant. 中國餐廳。

(B) Italian restaurant. 義大利餐廳。

(C) Fast-food restaurant. 速食餐廳。

* ready (ˈrɛdɪ) *adj.* 準備好的　　order (ˈɔrdɚ) *v.* 點菜

cheeseburger (ˈtʃizˌbɝgɚ) *n.* 起司漢堡

Coke (kok) *n.* 可口可樂　　***for here*** 內用

to go 外帶　　restaurant (ˈrɛstərənt) *n.* 餐廳

Chinese (tʃaɪˈniz) *adj.* 中國的

Italian (ɪˈtæljən) *adj.* 義大利的

fast-food (ˈfæstˌfud) *adj.* 速食的

TEST 2

第一部分：辨識句意（第 1-10 題，共 10 題）

作答說明： 第 1-10 題每題均有三個選項，請依據所聽到的單句，選出
符合描述的圖片。

示例題：你會看到

(A)   (B)   (C)

依據所播放的內容，正確答案應該選 A，請將答案紙該題「Ⓐ」
的地方塗黑、塗滿，即 ●ⒷⒸ。

1. (A)   (B)   (C)

2. (A)   (B)   (C)

3. (A)　　　(B)　　　(C)

4. (A)　　　(B)　　　(C)

5. (A)　　　(B)　　　(C)

6. (A)　　　(B)　　　(C)

7. (A)　　　(B)　　　(C)

8. (A)   (B)   (C)

9. (A)   (B)   (C)

10. (A)   (B)   (C)

第二部分：基本問答（第 11-20 題，共 10 題）

作答說明： 第 11-20 題每題均有三個選項，請依據所聽到的對話問句，選出一個最適合的回答。

示例題：你會看到

(A) She is talking to the teacher.

(B) She is a student in my class.

(C) She is wearing a beautiful dress.

依據所播放的內容，正確答案應該選 B，請將答案紙該題「Ⓑ」的地方塗黑、塗滿，即 Ⓐ ● Ⓒ 。

---

11. (A) Please. It's my treat.

   (B) Is it a trick? Don't move.

   (C) I can't complain. How about you?

12. (A) Two years old.

   (B) Six feet across.

   (C) One hundred dollars.

13. (A) She might be stuck in traffic.

   (B) We have failed in our mission.

   (C) Meet me at seven.

14. (A) Yes, I did.

   (B) Sometimes it lasts even longer.

   (C) It's OK.

15. (A) OK, but bring it back. Otherwise, you'll owe me another umbrella.

   (B) No, it doesn't matter. We can't all fit in that tiny car.

   (C) Only if it will make you happy. Take all of it.

16. (A) Good for her. Maybe now he'll show some respect.

   (B) Good job! Looks like all that hard work paid off.

   (C) Good grief! Now I have to clean up your mess.

17. (A) Yes. And I got his license plate number.
    (B) Wait until the light turns yellow, and then step on it.
    (C) The bus stops over there.

18. (A) He's an architect.
    (B) He's doing just fine.
    (C) Corporate lawyers.

19. (A) Buy a ticket. The next train leaves at four-thirty.
    (B) Donald Trump. He's a national treasure.
    (C) Take a right at the next corner. The station is on your right.

20. (A) I wouldn't know.
    (B) I know I wouldn't.
    (C) I wouldn't if I had known.

第三部分：言談理解（第 21-30 題，共 10 題）

作答說明：第 21-30 題每題均有三個選項，請依據所聽到的對話或短文內容，選出一個最適合的答案。

示例題：你會看到

(A) 9:50.　　(B) 10:00.　　(C) 10:10.

依據所播放的內容，正確答案應該選 B，請將答案紙該題「Ⓑ」的地方塗黑、塗滿，即 Ⓐ ● Ⓒ。

21. (A) Attend a concert.
    (B) Watch a sporting event.
    (C) Go shopping.

22. (A) Tuesday.
    (B) Wednesday.
    (C) Thursday.

23. (A) Dennis' ancestry.
    (B) Dennis' birthday present.
    (C) Dennis' retirement party.

24. (A) The men's room is far away.
    (B) The men's room is crowded.
    (C) The men's room is 20 minutes from here.

25. (A) Their weekend plans.
    (B) A picnic.
    (C) Their wedding invitations.

26. (A) In a toy store.
    (B) In Australia.
    (C) In a bank.

27. (A) At home.
    (B) At school.
    (C) At work.

28. (A) She's drunk plenty of coffee.
    (B) She's sitting on the edge of her desk.
    (C) She's afraid of falling asleep.

29. (A) Brother–sister.
    (B) Supervisor–employee.
    (C) Doctor–patient.

30. (A) Go for a walk.
    (B) Burn each other with cigarettes.
    (C) Play a game of chess.

TEST 2 詳解

第一部分：辨識句意

1. (**B**) (A) (B) (C)

The girl is reading a book. 女孩正在讀一本書。

* read〔rid〕v. 閱讀

2. (**B**) (A) (B) (C)

The man is smoking a pipe. 男子正在抽煙斗。

* smoke〔smok〕v. 吸；抽　　pipe〔paip〕n. 煙斗

3. (**C**) (A) (B) (C)

Oliver is playing his trumpet. 奧利佛正在吹喇叭。

* play〔ple〕v. 演奏；吹奏
trumpet〔'trʌmpɪt〕n. 喇叭；小號

4. (**C**) (A)  (B) (C)

Frank took third place in the spelling bee.

法蘭克在拼字比賽得到第三名。

* ***third place*** 第三名　　spelling〔'spɛlɪŋ〕*n.* 拼字
  bee〔bi〕*n.* 蜜蜂；（工作、娛樂等）聚會
  spelling bee 拼字比賽

5. (**C**) (A)  (B)  (C)

Harry is lifting weights. 哈利正在舉重。

* lift〔lɪft〕*v.* 舉起　　weight〔wet〕*n.* 重物

6. (**C**) (A)  (B)  (C)

The woman is cooking dinner. 女士正在煮晚餐。

* cook〔kʊk〕*v.* 煮　　dinner〔'dɪnɚ〕*n.* 晚餐

7. (**C**) (A)  (B)  (C)

There is a full moon tonight. 今晚有滿月。

* *full moon* 滿月

8. (**A**) (A)  (B)  (C)

This is a submarine. 這是潛水艇。

* submarine〔ˌsʌbməˈrin〕*n.* 潛水艇

9. (**B**) (A)  (B)  (C)

The couple is getting married.

這一對男女要結婚了。

* couple〔ˈkʌpḷ〕*n.* 一對男女
　get married 結婚

10. (**C**) (A) (B) (C)

The refrigerator door is wide open. 冰箱門大大地開著。

* refrigerator〔rɪˋfrɪdʒə,retə〕*n.* 冰箱（= *fridge*）
  wide〔waɪd〕*adv.* 張大地；充分張開地
  wide open 大大地開著的；敞開的

第二部分：基本問答

11. (**C**) Hi, Oscar. Long time no see. How's life been treating you?

嗨，奧斯卡。好久不見。你日子過得如何？

(A) Please. It's my treat. 拜託。這次我請客。

(B) Is it a trick? Don't move. 這是什麼花招？別動。

(C) I can't complain. How about you?

我沒什麼好抱怨的。你呢？

* *Long time no see*. 好久不見。
  treat〔trit〕*v.* 對待 *n.* 請客
  How's life been treating you? 你日子過得如何？
    (= *How are you doing?*)
  It's my treat. 我請客。(= *It's on me*.)
  trick〔trɪk〕*n.* 詭計；花招 complain〔kəmˋplen〕*v.* 抱怨
  I can't complain. 我沒什麼好抱怨的；我感到很滿意。【詳見背景說明】 *How about you?* 那你呢？

12. (**C**) I'm interested in this vacuum cleaner. How much is it?

我對這個吸塵器有興趣。多少錢？

(A) Two years old. 兩歲。

(B) Six feet across. 六呎寬。

(C) One hundred dollars. 一百元。

* interested〔'ɪntrɪstɪd〕*adj.* 感興趣的 < *in* >
vacuum〔'vækjuəm〕*n.* 吸塵器 (= *vacuum cleaner*)
foot〔fʊt〕*n.* 呎;英尺【一英尺為 30.48 公分】
across〔ə'krɔs〕*adv.* 寬…

13. (**A**) Why isn't Mary here? We can't start the meeting without
her. 為什麼瑪麗不在這裡?沒有她我們無法開會。

(A) She might be stuck in traffic. 她可能遇到塞車。

(B) We have failed in our mission. 我們的任務失敗了。

(C) Meet me at seven. 七點來見我。

* meeting〔'mitɪŋ〕*n.* 會議　　without〔wɪ'ðaʊt〕*prep.* 沒有
stuck〔stʌk〕*adj.* 困住的　　traffic〔'træfɪk〕*n.* 交通
fail〔fel〕*v.* 失敗 < *in* >　　mission〔'mɪʃən〕*n.* 任務
meet〔mit〕*v.* 和~見面

14. (**C**) Wow, four years is a long time. Do you like living in
Taipei? 哇,四年很長。你喜歡住在台北嗎?

(A) Yes, I did. 是的,我做了。

(B) Sometimes it lasts even longer. 有時候會持續更久。

(C) It's OK. 還可以。

* last〔læst〕*v.* 持續　　even〔'ivən〕*adv.*【強調比較級】更加

15. (**A**) It's raining again. Can I borrow your umbrella?
又在下雨了。我能跟你借把雨傘嗎?

(A) OK, but bring it back. Otherwise, you'll owe me
another umbrella.

好的,但要拿回來。否則你就又欠我額外一把雨傘了。

(B) No, it doesn't matter. We can't all fit in that tiny car.

不，這不重要。我們全部無法擠進那台小車。

(C) Only if it will make you happy. Take all of it.

只要這可以讓你高興。全部拿走吧。

* rain〔ren〕*v.* 下雨　　borrow〔'baro〕*v.* 借（入）
umbrella〔ʌm'brɛlə〕*n.* 雨傘
otherwise〔'ʌðɚ,waɪz〕*adv.* 否則　　owe〔o〕*v.* 欠
matter〔'mætɚ〕*v.* 重要　　*fit in* 裝進；擠進
tiny〔'taɪnɪ〕*adj.* 很小的　　*only if* 只要

16. (**B**) My grades are here. Looks like I got all As again!

我拿到成績了。看來我又拿了全 A！

(A) Good for her. Maybe now he'll show some respect.

真替她感到高興。或許現在他會表現出點尊重。

(B) Good job! Looks like all that hard work paid off.

做得好！看來所有的努力有了成果。

(C) Good grief! Now I have to clean up your mess.

天呀！現在我得收拾你的殘局。

* grade〔gred〕*n.* 分數；成績
Looks like~ 看來好像~（*= It looks like~*）
all As 全部甲等【As 是 A 的複數型，也可寫成 A's】
Good for sb. 真替某人感到高興。
maybe〔'mebɪ〕*adv.* 或許；可能　　show〔ʃo〕*v.* 展現；表現
respect〔rɪ'spɛkt〕*n.* 尊重　　*Good job!* 做得好！
hard work 努力　　*pay off* 有成果；成功
grief〔grif〕*n.* 悲傷
Good grief! 天呀；真不幸！【用於表示驚訝、憤怒】
clean up 清理　　mess〔mɛs〕*n.* 混亂；麻煩

17. (**A**) Did you see that truck run the red light? He could have killed someone.

你有看到那卡車闖紅燈嗎？他可能會撞死人。

(A) Yes. And I got his license plate number.

有。我有抄下他的車牌號碼。

(B) Wait until the light turns yellow, and then step on it.

等到變黃燈，然後踩油門。

(C) The bus stops over there. 公車停在那邊。

* truck〔trʌk〕*n.* 卡車　　***run the red light*** 闖紅燈
could have* + *p.p. 原本可能～
kill〔kɪl〕*v.* 殺死　　license〔'laɪsn̩s〕*n.* 執照；牌照
plate〔plet〕*n.* (汽車) 號碼牌　　***license plate*** 汽車車牌
turn〔tɜn〕*v.* 轉變成　　step〔stɛp〕*v.* 踩；踏
step on it 開快點；踩油門 (= *step on the gas*)
over there 在那裡

18. (**A**) I see. And what does your husband do for a living?

我了解了。那妳的丈夫靠什麼謀生？

(A) He's an architect. 他是位建築師。

(B) He's doing just fine. 他過得很好。

(C) Corporate lawyers. 企業律師。

* see〔si〕*v.* 明白；了解　　***I see.*** 我了解了。
do…for a living 做…而謀生
architect〔'ɑrkə,tɛkt〕*n.* 建築師
just〔dʒʌst〕*adv.* 完全；真地
be doing fine 過得好；順利 (= *be doing well*)
corporate〔'kɔrpərɪt〕*adj.* 公司的；企業的
lawyer〔'lɔjɚ〕*n.* 律師
corporate lawyer 企業律師【企業法律顧問】

19. (**C**) How do we get to the train station from here?

我們要如何從這裡到火車站？

(A) Buy a ticket. The next train leaves at four-thirty.

買車票。下一班火車四點三十分開。

(B) Donald Trump. He's a national treasure.

唐納德・川普。他是國家的珍寶。

(C) Take a right at the next corner. The station is on

your right. 在下個街角右轉。車站就在你的右手邊。

* **get to** 到達　　station〔'steʃən〕*n.* 車站

ticket〔'tɪkɪt〕*n.* 車票　　leave〔liv〕*v.* 離開；出發

Donald Trump〔'danḷd 'trʌmp〕*n.* 唐納德・川普【川普集團董

事長及總裁】　　national〔'næʃənḷ〕*adj.* 國家的

treasure〔'trɛʒɚ〕*n.* 寶藏；；寶貴的人；難得的人

take a right 向右轉 (= *make a right*)

corner〔'kɔrnɚ〕*n.* 街角　　**on the right** 在右邊

20. (**A**) Do you know if Tom is coming to the party tonight?

你知道湯姆今晚是否會來派對嗎？

(A) I wouldn't know. 我不可能知道。

(B) I know I wouldn't. 我知道我不會。

(C) I wouldn't if I had known.

如果當時我知道，我不會這麼做。

* if〔ɪf〕*conj.* 是否　　party〔'partɪ〕*n.* 派對

I wouldn't know. 我不可能知道。(= *There is no way that I*

would know the answer.)

第三部分：言談理解

21. (**B**) W：That was quite an exciting game!

女：那真是個刺激的比賽！

M：I know. Too bad our team lost, though.

男：我知道。不過可惜的是，我們的隊輸了。

W：That's OK. We'll get 'em next time.

女：沒關係。我們下次會報仇。

Question : What did the speakers just do?

說話者剛剛做了什麼事？

(A) Attend a concert. 去看演唱會。

(B) Watch a sporting event. 看運動比賽。

(C) Go shopping. 去購物。

* quite〔kwaɪt〕*adv.* 相當
exciting〔ɪk'saɪtɪŋ〕*adj.* 令人興奮的；刺激的
game〔gem〕*n.* 比賽
too bad 可惜的是 (= *It's too bad* (that)...)
lost〔lɔst〕*v.* 輸了【lose 的過去式】
though〔ðo〕*adv.*【置於句尾】可是；然而；不過 (= *however*)
get〔gɛt〕*v.* 殺死；懲罰 (= *punish*)
get 'em 懲罰他們 (= *punish them*)；報復他們 (= *take revenge on them*)　　attend〔ə'tɛnd〕*v.* 出席；參加
event〔ɪ'vɛnt〕*n.* 事件；(運動) 項目
sporting event 運動比賽

22. (**C**) M : Could I catch a ride downtown with you tomorrow morning, Rita?

男：瑞塔，我明天早上可以跟搭妳的便車到市中心嗎？

W : I'm afraid not, Steve. Tomorrow is my day off.

女：史蒂夫，恐怕不行。明天我休假。

M : Oh, that's right. I forgot that it's only Wednesday.

男：喔，沒錯。我忘了今天才星期三。

Question : When is the Rita's day off? 瑞塔星期幾休假？

(A) Tuesday. 星期二。　　　(B) Wednesday. 星期三。

(C) Thursday. 星期四。

* ride〔raɪd〕*n.* 搭車　　***catch a ride*** 搭便車【詳見背景說明】
downtown〔'daʊn,taʊn〕*adv.* 到市中心
I'm afraid not. 恐怕不行。　　off〔ɔf〕*adj.* 休息的

23. (**B**) W：Have you bought a birthday present for Dennis yet?

女：你買了生日禮物給丹尼斯了嗎？

M：No, I haven't. Have you?

男：不，還沒。妳買了嗎？

W：Not yet. Maybe we could go Dutch on something for him.

女：還沒。或許我們可以分攤買東西給他。

Question：What are the speakers discussing?

　　　　　　說話者在討論什麼？

(A) Dennis' ancestry. 丹尼斯的祖先。

(B) Dennis' birthday present. 丹尼斯的生日禮物。

(C) Dennis' retirement party. 丹尼斯的退休派對。

* bought〔bɔt〕*v.* 買【buy 的過去分詞】
present〔'prɛznt〕*n.* 禮物　　yet〔jɛt〕*adv.*【用於疑問句】已經
go Dutch 各付各的；分攤＜ *on* ＞
discuss〔dɪ'skʌs〕*v.* 討論　　ancestry〔'ænsɛstrɪ〕*n.* 祖先
retirement〔rɪ'taɪrmənt〕*n.* 退休

24. (**A**) M：Where is the men's room?

男：請問男廁在哪裡？

W：Take the escalator up to the second level, turn right, walk 50 meters and make another right. It's across from Macy's.

女：搭電扶梯往上到二樓，右轉，走五十公尺後再右轉。在梅西百貨的對面。

M：If I'm not back in 20 minutes, send the search and rescue team!

男：如果我二十分鐘後沒回來，請派搜救隊！

Question：What does the man mean? 男士的意思是什麼？

(A) The men's room is far away. 男廁很遠。

(B) The men's room is crowded. 男廁很擁擠。

(C) The men's room is 20 minutes from here.

男廁離這裡有二十分鐘路程。

* ***men's room*** 男生廁所　　escalator〔ˋɛskəˏletɚ〕*n.* 電扶梯
level〔ˋlɛv!〕*n.* 層　　meter〔ˋmitɚ〕*n.* 公尺
across from 在…的對面
Macy's 梅西百貨公司【美國的連鎖百貨公司】
send〔sɛnd〕*v.* 派遣　　search〔sɝtʃ〕*n.* 尋找；搜查
rescue〔ˋrɛskju〕*n.* 救援　　***search and rescue team*** 搜救隊
crowded〔ˋkraʊdɪd〕*adj.* 擁擠的

25. (**B**) M : The weather report said it will rain this afternoon.

男：天氣預報說今天下午會下雨。

W : Oh, no! Do you think they will cancel the picnic?

女：喔，不！你覺得他們會取消野餐嗎？

M : Probably not. The invitation says "Rain or shine."

男：可能不會。邀請函說「無論晴雨」。

Question : What are the speakers discussing?

說話者在討論什麼？

(A) Their weekend plans. 他們週末的計畫。

(B) A picnic. 野餐。

(C) Their wedding invitations. 他們的喜帖。

* ***weather report*** 天氣預報　　cancel〔ˋkæns!〕*v.* 取消
picnic〔ˋpɪknɪk〕*n.* 野餐　　probably〔ˋprɑbəblɪ〕*adv.* 可能
invitation〔ˏɪnvəˋteʃən〕*n.* 邀請函　　***rain or shine*** 無論晴雨
weekend〔ˋwikˏɛnd〕*n.* 週末　　plan〔plæn〕*n.* 計畫
wedding〔ˋwɛdɪŋ〕*n.* 婚禮　　***wedding invitation*** 喜帖

26. (**C**) W : I'd like to wire some money back to Australia. Can
I do that here?

女：我想要匯些錢回澳洲。我可以在這裡匯嗎？

M : Do you have an account with us? Otherwise there will be a processing fee.

男：妳有我們的帳戶嗎？否則會有手續費。

W : No, I don't have an account in this country. But I'd still like to wire the money.

女：沒有，我在這國家沒有帳戶，但我還是想要匯款。

Question : Where did this conversation take place?

這對話發生在哪裡？

(A) In a toy store. 在玩具店。

(B) In Australia. 在澳洲。

(C) In a bank. 在銀行。

* *would like to V.* 想要～　　wire〔waɪr〕*v.* 電匯（錢）
Australia〔ɔ'steljə〕*n.* 澳洲　　account〔ə'kaʊnt〕*n.* 帳戶
otherwise〔'ʌðə‚waɪz〕*adv.* 否則
process〔'prɑsɛs〕*v.* 處理　　fee〔fi〕*n.* 費用
processing fee 手續費
conversation〔‚kɑnvə'seʃən〕*n.* 對話
would like to V. 想要　　*take place* 發生
bank〔bæŋk〕*n.* 銀行

27.(**C**) W : Did John say what time he'd be here?

女：約翰有說他幾點會到這裡嗎？

M : He said he'd come as soon as he got off work.

男：他說他一下班就會過來。

W : Hmm, OK. Well, the store closes in an hour, so…

女：嗯，好的。嗯，商店一小時後就要關了，所以…

Question : Where is John now? 約翰現在在哪？

(A) At home. 在家裡。

(B) At school. 在學校。

(C) At work. 在工作。

* ***as soon as*** 一…就　　***get off work*** 下班
hmm〔m〕*interj.* 嗯【表示疑慮或猶豫所發出的聲音】
at work 在工作

28. (**A**) M：Would you like some more coffee? I'm going to brew another pot.

男：妳想要再喝點咖啡嗎？我要再泡一壺。

W：No thanks, Leon. Another cup might put me over the edge.

女：不，謝謝，里安。再喝一杯會超出我所能負荷。

M：Not me. I can't seem to wake up this morning.

男：我沒有這問題。我今天早上似乎無法清醒過來。

Question：What does the woman imply?

女士暗示什麼？

(A) She's drunk plenty of coffee. 她已經喝了很多咖啡。

(B) She's sitting on the edge of her desk.
她正坐在她辦公桌的邊緣。

(C) She's afraid of falling asleep. 她害怕睡著。

* brew〔bru〕*v.* 泡（咖啡、茶）
pot〔pat〕*n.* 一壺的量　　edge〔edʒ〕*n.* 刀口；邊緣
put sb. over the edge 使某人無法承受【詳見背景說明】
seem〔sim〕*v.* 似乎　　***wake up*** 醒來
imply〔ɪm'plaɪ〕*v.* 暗示　　***plenty of*** 很多
be afraid of 害怕　　***fall asleep*** 睡著

29. (**B**) W：Sorry I'm late, Mr. Peabody. There was an accident in the subway and…

女：抱歉，我遲到了，皮博迪先生。地鐵上出了意外而且…。

M：That's OK, Marcy. Just don't let it happen again.

男：瑪西，沒關係。就不要再讓這種事情發生就好。

W : I won't. Thank you for being so understanding.

女：我不會的。謝謝你的諒解。

Question : What is the relationship between Mr. Peabody
　　　　　　and Marcy? 皮博迪先生和瑪西是什麼關係？

(A) Brother–sister. 兄妹。

(B) Supervisor–employee. 主管和員工。

(C) Doctor–patient. 醫生和病人。

* late〔let〕*adj.* 遲到的　　　accident〔'æksədənt〕*n.* 意外
　subway〔'sʌb,we〕*n.* 地鐵　　***That's OK.*** 沒關係。
　happen〔'hæpən〕*v.* 發生
　understanding〔,ʌndə'stændɪŋ〕*adj.* 體諒的；明理的
　relationship〔rɪ'leʃən,ʃɪp〕*n.* 關係
　supervisor〔'supə,vaɪzə〕*n.* 主管
　employee〔,ɛmplɔɪ'i〕*n.* 員工　　patient〔'peʃənt〕*n.* 病人

30. (**C**)　M : I'm bored. Want to play a game?

男：我好無聊。想要玩個遊戲嗎？

W : Sure. What are we going to play?

女：當然。我們要玩什麼？

M : How about chess?

男：西洋棋如何？

Question : What will the speakers most likely do next?
　　　　　　說話者接下來最可能做什麼？

(A) Go for a walk. 去散步。

(B) Burn each other with cigarettes. 用香菸燙彼此。

(C) Play a game of chess. 下西洋棋。

* bored〔bord〕*adj.* 無聊的　　***How about ~?*** ～如何？
　likely〔'laɪklɪ〕*adv.* 可能　　next〔nɛkst〕*adv.* 接下來
　go for a walk 去散步　　burn〔bɜn〕*v.* 燒；燙
　each other 彼此；互相　　cigarette〔'sɪgə,rɛt〕*n.* 香菸

TEST 3

第一部分：辨識句意（第 1-10 題，共 10 題）

作答說明： 第 1-10 題每題均有三個選項，請依據所聽到的單句，選出符合描述的圖片。

示例題：你會看到

(A)　　　　　　　(B)　　　　　　　(C)

依據所播放的內容，正確答案應該選 A，請將答案紙該題「(A)」的地方塗黑、塗滿，即 ●(B)(C)。

1. (A)　　　　(B)　　　　(C)

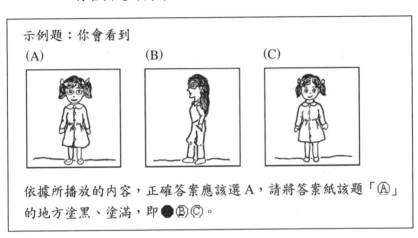

2. (A)　　　　(B)　　　　(C)

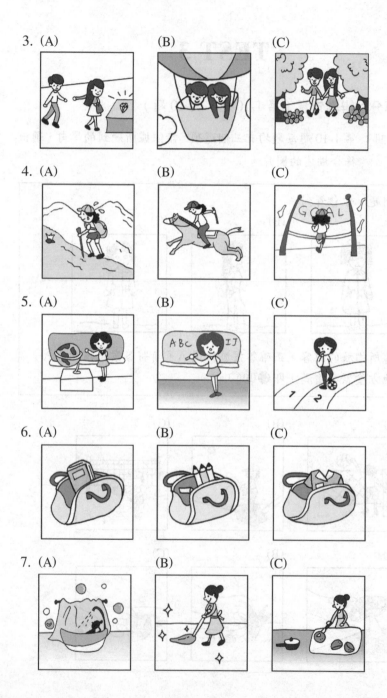

8. (A)　　　　　(B)　　　　　(C)

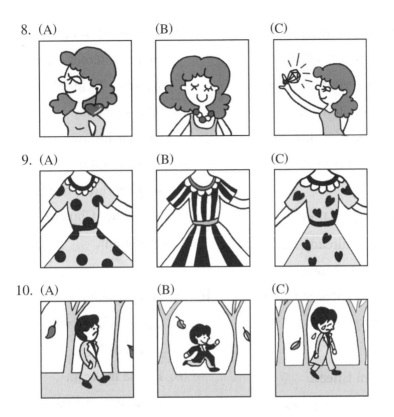

9. (A)　　　　　(B)　　　　　(C)

10. (A)　　　　　(B)　　　　　(C)

第二部分：基本問答（第 11-20 題，共 10 題）

作答說明： 第 11-20 題每題均有三個選項，請依據所聽到的對話問句，選出一個最適合的回答。

示例題：你會看到

(A) She is talking to the teacher.

(B) She is a student in my class.

(C) She is wearing a beautiful dress.

依據所播放的內容，正確答案應該選 B，請將答案紙該題「Ⓑ」的地方塗黑、塗滿，即Ⓐ●Ⓒ。

---

11. (A) No, your directions were excellent.
    (B) No, your directions were terrible.
    (C) No, your directions were ignored.

12. (A) I will, Mom.
    (B) I've already fed them, Mom.
    (C) I let them out an hour ago.

13. (A) I'm fifteen.
    (B) Search engines.
    (C) Make it more like eight years, Dick.

14. (A) You are a nice person.
    (B) Green.
    (C) Chocolate, I guess.

15. (A) I get most of my news on the Internet—ever heard of Twitter?
    (B) That—and the mother-in-law.
    (C) Just what the neighborhood needs —another Chinese restaurant.

16. (A) Have a seat and the doctor will be with you shortly.
    (B) Please make an appointment first.
    (C) Oh, that's too bad.

17. (A) Put the ball in the basket, son.
    (B) Yes, give me one of those fruit pies.
    (C) No, I'll do it later.

18. (A) Just under 75 kilos.

    (B) German and Italian.

    (C) Twenty-five.

19. (A) If you don't mind, I'll hold on to it, thanks.

    (B) You should learn how to take a compliment.

    (C) Come to my house for dinner.

20. (A) I'd be happy to open the window for you.

    (B) I'd be happy to sweep the floor for you.

    (C) I'd be happy to take care of that for you.

第三部分：言談理解（第 21-30 題，共 10 題）

作答説明： 第 21-30 題每題均有三個選項，請依據所聽到的對話或短文內容，選出一個最適合的答案。

示例題：你會看到

(A) 9:50.　　(B) 10:00.　　(C) 10:10.

依據所播放的內容，正確答案應該選 B，請將答案紙該題「Ⓑ」的地方塗黑、塗滿，即Ⓐ●Ⓒ。

---

21. (A) A complicated math problem.

    (B) A marine animal.

    (C) A cooking method.

22. (A) Teacher–student.

    (B) Supervisor–employee.

    (C) Husband–wife.

23. (A) To a concert.
    (B) To a driving lesson.
    (C) To a shopping mall.

24. (A) She wants to watch
        a television show.
    (B) She isn't feeling
        very well.
    (C) She made plans to
        go out with her
        friends.

25. (A) In a drugstore.
    (B) In a library.
    (C) In a restaurant.

26. (A) Enthusiastic.
    (B) Scornful.
    (C) Anxious.

27. (A) Booking a hotel room.
    (B) Making a reservation at
        a restaurant.
    (C) Cancelling a
        subscription.

28. (A) Building a relationship.
    (B) Meeting a friend.
    (C) Ordering a cup of coffee.

29. (A) He is a fast learner.
    (B) He is a religious man.
    (C) He is in the hospital.

30. (A) The man should seek
        professional help.
    (B) The man should get
        organized.
    (C) The man should take
        better care of his dog.

TEST 3 詳解

第一部分：辨識句意

1. (**C**) (A)   (B)   (C)

The boy is playing tennis. 男孩正在打網球。

* tennis〔ˈtɛnɪs〕*n.* 網球

2. (**A**) (A)   (B)   (C)

This is a mushroom. 這是蘑菇。

* mushroom〔ˈmʌʃrum〕*n.* 蘑菇

3. (**C**) (A)   (B)   (C)

They are walking through the park. 他們正步行經過公園。

* walk〔wɔk〕*v.* 步行；走路
   through〔θru〕*prep.* 經過；通過

4. (**A**) (A)　　　　　　(B)　　　　　　(C)

She is hiking up a mountain. 她正在登山。

5. (**B**) (A)　　　　　　(B)　　　　　　(C)

She is an English teacher. 她是一位英文老師。

＊ teacher (ˈtitʃɚ) *n.* 老師

6. (**C**) (A)　　　　　　(B)　　　　　　(C)

There is a shirt in the handbag.

手提袋裡有一件襯衫。

＊ shirt (ʃɝt) *n.* 襯衫
　 handbag (ˈhænd,bæg) *n.* 手提包；手提袋

7. (**A**) (A) (B)  (C)

The woman is taking a bath. 女士正在洗澡。

* bath〔bæθ〕 *n.* 洗澡　　***take a bath*** 洗澡

8. (**C**) (A)  (B)  (C)

Marilou is proud of her new ring.

瑪莉露對她的新戒指感到很驕傲。

* ***be proud of*** 對～感到驕傲　　ring〔rɪŋ〕 *n.* 戒指

9. (**A**) (A)  (B)  (C)

Laura's polka dot dress is very cute.

蘿拉的圓點花樣洋裝很可愛。

* dot〔dɑt〕 *n.* 點　　***polka dot*** 圓點花樣
　dress〔drɛs〕 *n.* 洋裝　　cute〔kjut〕 *adj.* 可愛的

10. (**B**) (A) 　　(B) 　　(C)

John is running through the forest. 約翰正跑步穿越森林。

* through〔θru〕*prep.* 穿過　　forest〔'fɔrɪst〕*n.* 森林

第二部分：基本問答

11. (**A**) Please come in. Did you have any trouble finding the place? 請進。你找這個地方有遇到什麼困難嗎？

(A) No, your directions were excellent.
不，你的指引很棒。

(B) No, your directions were terrible.
不，你的指引很糟糕。

(C) No, your directions were ignored.
不，你的指引被忽略了。

* *have trouble + V-ing* 做…有困難
directions〔də'rɛkʃəns〕*n. pl.* 指引；指示
exellent〔'ɛksḷənt〕*adj.* 極好的；很棒的
terrible〔'tɛrəbḷ〕*adj.* 很糟的　　ignore〔ɪg'nor〕*v.* 忽視

12. (**B**) Billy, it's Mom. Don't forget to feed Fred and Max.
比利，是媽。別忘了要餵弗瑞德和麥克斯。

(A) I will, Mom. 我會的，媽。

(B) I've already fed them, Mom. 我已經餵他們了，媽。

(C) I let them out an hour ago. 我一小時前有放牠們出來。

* feed〔fid〕*v.* 餵【三態為：feed-fed-fed】
let ~ out 放出去~

13. (**C**) It's so good to see you, Mark. It's been what, six years already? 看到你眞好，馬克。已經六年沒看到你了吧？

　　(A) I'm fifteen. 我十五歲。

　　(B) Search engines. 搜尋引擎。

　　(C) Make it more like eight years, Dick.
　　　　我覺得好像有八年了，狄克。

　　* what〔hwɑt〕*interj.* 哦【用於想數字或數量而暫停】
　　　 search〔sɝtʃ〕*n.* 搜尋　　 engine〔'ɛndʒən〕*n.* 引擎
　　　 Make it more like eight years. 覺得好像有八年了。【詳見背景說明】

14. (**C**) What's your favorite flavor of ice cream?
　　你最喜歡的冰淇淋口味是什麼？

　　(A) You are a nice person. 你是一個好人。

　　(B) Green. 綠色。

　　(C) Chocolate, I guess. 我想是巧克力。

　　* favorite〔'fevərɪt〕*adj.* 最喜歡的　　 flavor〔'flevɚ〕*n.* 味道
　　　 ice cream 冰淇淋　　 guess〔gɛs〕*v.* 猜想；認爲

15. (**C**) There's a new Chinese restaurant on Seventh Street.
　　Want to go check it out?
　　在第七街有一家新的中式餐廳。要去看看嗎？

　　(A) I get most of my news on the Internet—ever heard of Twitter? 我大多的新聞都從網路上得知—聽過推特嗎？

　　(B) That—and the mother-in-law. 那位—還有岳母。

　　(C) Just what the neighborhood needs—another Chinese restaurant. 那就是這附近需要的—另一間中式餐廳。

　　* Chinese〔tʃaɪ'niz〕*adj.* 中國的；中式的
　　　 restaurant〔'rɛstərənt〕*n.* 餐廳　　 ***go + V.*** 去～ (= *go to V.*)
　　　 check out 檢查；看看　　 Internet〔'ɪntɚˌnɛt〕*n.* 網路

hear of 聽過

Twitter〔'twɪtɚ〕*n.* 推特【一個社交網絡，此字原意爲「吱吱叫」】

mother-in-law 岳母；婆婆

neighborhood〔'nebɚ,hʊd〕*n.* 附近地區

16. (**A**) Yes, I have an appointment with Dr. Frink. It's for my
son, George.

是的，我和弗林克醫生有約。是替我兒子喬治約的。

(A) Have a seat and the doctor will be with you shortly.
請坐，醫生馬上就過來。

(B) Please make an appointment first. 請先預約。

(C) Oh, that's too bad. 喔，那眞是太可惜了。

* appointment〔ə'pɔɪntmənt〕*n.* 約會；約診
seat〔sit〕*n.* 座位　　**have a seat** 坐下；就座
shortly〔'ʃɔrtlɪ〕*adv.* 不久；很快地
make an appointment 預約　　**That's too bad.** 眞可惜。

17. (**B**) Two Big Smacks, medium fries and a large Jolt cola.
Anything else?

兩個大麥片，中薯，以及一杯大焦特可樂。還需要什麼嗎？

(A) Put the ball in the basket, son. 把球放在籃子裡，兒子。

(B) Yes, give me one of those fruit pies.
是的，給我那種的水果派一塊。

(C) No, I'll do it later. 不，我晚點會做。

* Smack〔smæk〕*n.* 麥片【品牌名】
medium〔'midɪəm〕*adj.* 中等的
fries〔fraɪz〕*n. pl.* 薯條　　large〔lardʒ〕*adj.* 大的
jolt〔dʒolt〕*n.* 上下劇烈搖動　　**Jolt cola** 焦特可樂
basket〔'bæskɪt〕*n.* 籃子　　**fruit pie** 水果派
later〔'letɚ〕*adv.* 之後

18. (**C**) Happy Birthday, Mike! How old are you now?
生日快樂，麥克！你現在幾歲？

(A) Just under 75 kilos. 還不到 75 公斤。

(B) German and Italian. 德文和義大利文。

(C) Twenty-five. 二十五。

* kilo〔'kɪlo〕*n.* 公斤（= *kilogram*）
German〔'dʒɝmən〕*n.* 德文
Italian〔ɪ'tæljən〕*n.* 義大利文

19. (**A**) Thank you very much for coming. May I take your coat?
很謝謝你來。可以幫你拿外套嗎？

(A) If you don't mind, I'll hold on to it, thanks.
如果你不介意，我要自己拿著，謝謝。

(B) You should learn how to take a compliment.
你應該學著如何接受讚美。

(C) Come to my house for dinner. 來我家吃晚餐。

* coat〔kot〕*n.* 外套　　mind〔maɪnd〕*v.* 介意
hold on to 抓住；留著
compliment〔'kɑmpləmənt〕*n.* 稱讚

20. (**C**) I'm going on vacation next week and I need someone to
water my plants.
我下週要去度假，而我需要有人幫我替植物澆水。

(A) I'd be happy to open the window for you.
我會很高興可以幫你打開窗戶。

(B) I'd be happy to sweep the floor for you.
我會很高興可以幫你掃地。

(C) I'd be happy to take care of that for you.
我會很高興可以幫你處理那件事。

> * vacation〔vəˈkeʃən〕*n.* 休假　　***on vacation***　度假
> water〔ˈwɑtə〕*v.* 給…澆水　　plant〔plænt〕*n.* 植物
> open〔ˈopən〕*v.* 打開　　window〔ˈwɪndo〕*n.* 窗戶
> sweep〔swip〕*v.* 打掃　　floor〔flor〕*n.* 地板
> ***take care of***　照顧；處理

第三部分：言談理解

21. (**B**) W：Why do they call it an "octopus"?

　　　女：我們為什麼把牠叫作"octopus"？

　　　M：Because it's got eight arms, legs, or tentacles—whatever they're called.

　　　男：因為牠有八隻手臂、腳，或者說是觸角—不管它們是如何被稱呼。

　　　W：So where does the "pus" part come in? Why not call it an "octoarm"?

　　　女：所以需要 "pus" 這個部分做什麼？何不叫它作 "octoarm"？

　　　Question：What are the speakers mainly discussing?

　　　　　　　說話者在主要在討論什麼？

　　　(A) A complicated math problem.　一個複雜的數學問題。

　　　(B) A marine animal.　一個海洋動物。

　　　(C) A cooking method.　一個烹飪方式。

* octopus〔ˈɑktəpəs〕*n.* 章魚
　tentacle〔ˈtɛntəkḷ〕*n.* 觸手；觸角
　Where~comes in　需要~的地方；~可以發揮作用的地方
　　(= *What~is needed for*)
　come in　在~起作用 (= *play a role in*)
　Why not V.?　何不~　　mainly〔ˈmenlɪ〕*adv.* 主要地
　discuss〔dɪˈskʌs〕*v.* 討論
　complicated〔ˈkɑmpləˌketɪd〕*adj.* 複雜的
　marine〔məˈrin〕*adj.* 海洋的　　method〔ˈmɛθəd〕*n.* 方法

22. (**C**) M : Are you going to your book club meeting tonight?

男：妳今晚要去讀書會嗎？

W : No, I'm too tired. But don't let that stop you from hosting your poker game.

女：不，我太累了。但不要讓這件事情阻礙你舉辦撲克牌遊戲。

M : It won't. I'm asking because Todd is coming, and I know how you feel about him since he left Marie.

男：不會的。我在問是因為塔德要來，而我知道自從他離開瑪莉之後，妳對他的感覺。

Question : What is the most likely relationship between the speakers?

說話者最可能的關係是什麼？

(A) Teacher–student. 師生。

(B) Supervisor–employee. 主管和員工。

(C) Husband–wife. 夫妻。

* ***book club*** 書友會；讀書會
  meeting〔'mitɪŋ〕*n.* 會議；聚會
  tired〔taɪrd〕*adj.* 疲倦的；累的
  stop *sb.* ***from V-ing*** 使某人無法～
  host〔host〕*v.* 主辦　　poker〔'pokɚ〕*n.* 撲克牌
  likely〔'laɪklɪ〕*adj.* 可能的
  relationship〔rɪ'leʃən,ʃɪp〕*n.* 關係
  supervisor〔'supɚ,vaɪzɚ〕*n.* 主管
  employee〔,ɛmplɔɪ'i〕*n.* 員工

23. (**A**) M : You better take a jacket, honey. It's supposed to get down to the forties tonight.

男：妳最好帶件外套，親愛的。今晚溫度應該會下降到四十幾度（約攝氏四到五度）。

W : We're not going to be outside, Dad. We're going straight from the car to the concert.

女：我們不會在外面，爸爸。我們要直接從車裡面到演唱會。

M : Well, you never know. What if you have to wait in line?

男：嗯，很難說。萬一妳必須排隊呢？

Question : Where is the woman going tonight?

女士今晚要去哪？

(A) To a concert. 去演唱會。

(B) To a driving lesson. 去駕訓班。

(C) To a shopping mall. 去購物中心。

* ***You better V.*** 你最好～（= *You had better V.* ）
be supposed to V. 應該～　　***get down*** 下降
straight〔stret〕*adv.* 直接地　　concert〔'kɑnsɝt〕*n.* 演唱會
You never know. 很難說；世事難料。
What if～? 如果～該怎麼辦？　　***wait in line*** 排隊等候
driving lesson 駕訓課程；駕訓班
shopping mall 購物中心

24. (**A**) W : Sorry I can't come to your party tonight, Rick. It's the season finale of The Big Bang Theory and it's my all-time favorite show.

女：很抱歉我今晚無法去你的派對，瑞克。這是生活大爆炸這季的最後一集，而且它是我史上最喜歡的節目。

M : Well, couldn't you just record it on DVR and watch it after the party?

男：嗯，妳不能用數位錄影機錄下來，派對後再看嗎？

W : Of course not! Then I'll miss the excitement of being in the moment.

女：當然不行！那樣我就錯過了當下的刺激感。

Question：Why won't the woman attend the man's party?

爲何女士無法去男士的派對？

(A) She wants to watch a television show.

她想要看一個電視節目。

(B) She isn't feeling very well. 她覺得不太舒服。

(C) She made plans to go out with her friends.

他計畫要跟朋友出去。

* season〔'sizn〕*n.* 季；季節

finale〔fɪ'nɑlɪ〕*n.* 最後一集；終場

bang〔bæŋ〕*n.* 重及；巨響　　theory〔'θiərɪ〕*n.* 理論

The Big Bang Theory 生活大爆炸【美國 CBS（哥倫比亞廣播

公司）在 2007 年推出的情景喜劇】

all-time 前所未聞的；空前的

favorite〔'fevərɪt〕*adj.* 最喜歡的　　show〔ʃo〕*n.* 表演；節目

DVR 數位錄影機（*= digital video recorder*）

miss〔mɪs〕*v.* 錯過

excitement〔ɪk'saɪtmənt〕*n.* 興奮；刺激

moment〔'momənt〕*n.*（特定）時間

be in the moment 活在當下（*= live in the present*）

attend〔ə'tɛnd〕*v.* 出席；參加　　plan〔plæn〕*v.* 計畫；打算

25. (**A**) M：Have you got anything for acne?

男：你們有什麼可以治療痘痘的嗎？

W：We've got this herbal cream. It's great stuff. Made from mint. Highly recommended.

女：我們有這種草本軟膏。這是很棒的東西，用薄荷做的。非常

推薦。

M：OK, I'll try it. And how about something for muscle pain?

男：好的，我試看看。那有沒有治療肌肉痛的？

Question：Where is this conversation most likely taking

place？ 這對話最可能出現在哪裡？

(A) In a drugstore. 藥局裡。

(B) In a library. 圖書館裡。

(C) In a restaurant. 餐廳裡。

* acne〔'æknɪ〕*n.* 痘痘；粉刺

herbal〔'hɜbl̩〕*adj.* 草藥的；草本的

cream〔krim〕*n.* 乳膏　　stuff〔stʌf〕*n.* 東西

mint〔mɪnt〕*n.* 薄荷

highly〔'haɪlɪ〕*adv.* 非常

recommmend〔ˌrɛkə'mɛnd〕*v.* 推薦

How about~? ～如何？　　muscle〔'mʌsl̩〕*n.* 肌肉

pain〔pen〕*n.* 疼痛

conversation〔ˌkɑnvə'seʃən〕*n.* 對話

likely〔'laɪklɪ〕*adv.* 可能地　　***take place*** 發生

drugstore〔'drʌgˌstor〕*n.* 藥房

library〔'laɪˌbrɛrɪ〕*n.* 圖書館

26. (**B**)　W：Why do people insist on singing karaoke when they
cannot sing?

女：為什麼人們不會唱歌卻又堅持要唱卡拉 OK 呢？

M：It's fun, Julie. The point isn't to be Whitney Houston
or Wayne Newton up there. It's just a way to unwind
with your friends.

男：朱莉，這很有趣。重點不是要像惠妮休士頓或是韋恩牛頓在
舞台上表演一樣。這只是一個和你朋友一起放鬆的方法。

W：Well, I don't get it. I think it makes people look
foolish. How does that help someone unwind?

女：嗯，我不懂。我覺得這讓人看起來很可笑。那怎麼可以讓人
放鬆？

Question：Which description best matches the woman's attitude toward karaoke?

哪個敘述最符合女士對卡拉 OK 的看法？

(A) Enthusiastic. 有熱忱的。

(B) Scornful. 輕視的。

(C) Anxious. 焦慮的。

* insist〔ɪn'sɪst〕 *v.* 堅持 < on >
  karaoke〔ˌkɑrɑ'oke〕 *n.* 卡拉 OK　　fun〔fʌn〕 *adj.* 有趣的
  point〔pɔɪnt〕 *n.* 重點
  Whitney Houston 惠妮休士頓【美國女歌手】
  Wayne Newton 韋恩牛頓【美國男歌手】
  up there 在那裡；這裡指「在舞台上」(= *on the stage*)
  unwind〔ʌn'waɪnd〕 *v.* 使放鬆
  get〔gɛt〕 *v.* 了解；明白　　look〔lʊk〕 *v.* 看起來
  foolish〔'fulɪʃ〕 *adj.* 愚蠢的；可笑的
  description〔dɪ'skrɪpʃən〕 *n.* 敘述
  match〔mætʃ〕 *v.* 符合　　attitude〔'ætəˌtjud〕 *n.* 態度；看法
  toward〔tord〕 *prep.* 對於
  enthusiastic〔ɪnˌθuzɪ'æstɪk〕 *adj.* 充滿熱忱的
  scornful〔'skɔrnfəl〕 *adj.* 輕視的
  anxious〔'æŋkʃəs〕 *adj.* 焦慮的

27. (**B**) W：Thank you for calling Applebee's. How can I help you?

女：蘋果蜂蜜謝謝您的來電。我可以替您做什麼？

M：I'd like to reserve a table for eight o'clock on Friday night.

男：我想要預訂週五晚上八點的位子。

W：Your name and phone number, please?

女：請問您的姓名和電話是？

Question：What is the man doing？ 男士正在做什麼？

(A) Booking a hotel room. 預訂旅館的房間。

(B) Making a reservation at a restaurant. 預訂餐廳。

(C) Cancelling a subscription. 取消訂閱。

* *Applebee's* 蘋果蜂蜜餐廳【美式連鎖餐廳】
would like to V. 想要～　　reserve〔rɪ'zɝv〕*v.* 預訂
table〔'tebḷ〕*n.* 桌子；餐桌
reserve a table 預訂一桌的位子
book〔bʊk〕*v.* 預訂　　hotel〔ho'tɛl〕*n.* 飯店；旅館
reservation〔ˌrɛzɝ'veʃən〕*n.* 預訂
make a reservation 預訂
cancel〔'kænsḷ〕*v.* 取消
subscription〔səb'skrɪpʃən〕*n.* 訂閱

28. (**B**) W : Are you sure this is where Richard said we should meet him?

女：你確定這裡就是理查說我們要跟他會面的地方嗎？

M : Yes, I'm sure. This is the only Starbucks in Roseland, isn't it?

男：是的，我確定。這是羅斯蘭德唯一的星巴克，不是嗎？

W : No, there's another one over on Cherry Creek Road. I'd be willing to bet that's the Starbucks Richard was talking about.

女：不，在櫻桃溪路那裡還有一家。我願意賭看看那就是理查說的星巴克。

Question : What are the speakers doing?

　　　　說話者在做什麼？

(A) Building a relationship. 建立關係。

(B) Meeting a friend. 要和朋友見面。

(C) Ordering a cup of coffee. 點一杯咖啡。

* sure〔ʃʊr〕*adj.* 確定的　　meet〔mit〕*v.* 和～見面
　Starbucks 星巴克【連鎖咖啡店】
　Roseland〔'roz,lænd〕羅斯蘭德【位於新澤西州】
　cherry〔'tʃɛrɪ〕*n.* 櫻桃
　creek〔krik〕*n.* 小溪；小河
　willing〔'wɪlɪŋ〕*adj.* 願意的
　bet〔bɛt〕*v.* 打賭　　order〔'ɔrdɚ〕*v.* 點（菜）

29.(**C**) M：Hi, Tina.　How's Scooter doing?

男：嗨，蒂娜。史可達最近如何？

W：He's recovering a lot faster than the doctors thought.
　　He should be released from the hospital in a day or
　　two.

女：他恢復的比醫生認爲的還快。他應該一兩天後就可以出院了。

M：That's great news.　We'll keep ol' Scooter in our
　　prayers.

男：那眞是個好消息。我們會繼續爲老史可達祈禱。

Question：What do we know about Scooter?

　　　　　我們可以知道史可達怎麼了？

(A) He is a fast learner.　他學得很快。

(B) He is a religious man.　他是個虔誠的人。

(C) He is in the hospital.　他在住院。

* recover〔rɪ'kʌvɚ〕*v.* 復原
　a lot【強調比較級】非常
　release〔rɪ'lis〕*v.* 釋放
　be released from the hospital 出院
　ol' 老的（= *old*）　　prayer〔prɛr〕*n.* 祈禱
　keep sb. *in one's* ***prayers*** 替某人祈禱（= *pray for sb.*）
　learner〔'lɜnɚ〕*n.* 學習者
　religious〔rɪ'lɪdʒəs〕*adj.* 宗教的；虔誠的

30. (**B**) W : Did you remember Elaine's birthday this year?

女：你記得今年伊蓮的生日嗎？

M : No, and I'm still in the doghouse about our anniversary.

男：不記得，我還在因為忘了週年紀念日被冷落。

W : You should get a calendar so you can write down all these important dates.

女：你應該要有本行事曆，這樣你才能夠記下所有重要的日子。

Question : What does the woman suggest?

女士建議什麼？

(A) The man should seek professional help.

男士應該尋求專業協助。

(B) The man should get organized.

男士應該要有條理。

(C) The man should take better care of his dog.

男士應該多照顧他的狗。

* doghouse〔'dɔg,haʊs〕*n.* 狗屋

be in the doghouse （因做錯事）失寵的；被冷落的（ = *be in disfavor* ）

anniversary〔,ænə'vɜsərɪ〕*n.* 週年紀念日

calendar〔'kæləndɚ〕*n.* 行事曆

suggest〔səg'dʒɛst〕*v.* 建議

seek〔sik〕*v.* 尋求

professional〔prə'fɛʃənl̩〕*adj.* 專業的

organized〔'ɔrgən,aɪzd〕*adj.* 有組織的；有條理的

take care of 照顧

TEST 4

第一部分：辨識句意（第 1-10 題，共 10 題）

作答說明： 第 1-10 題每題均有三個選項，請依據所聽到的單句，選出符合描述的圖片。

示例題：你會看到

(A)   (B)   (C)

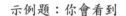

依據所播放的內容，正確答案應該選 A，請將答案紙該題「Ⓐ」的地方塗黑、塗滿，即 ●ⒷⒸ。

---

1. (A)   (B)   (C)

2. (A)   (B)   (C)

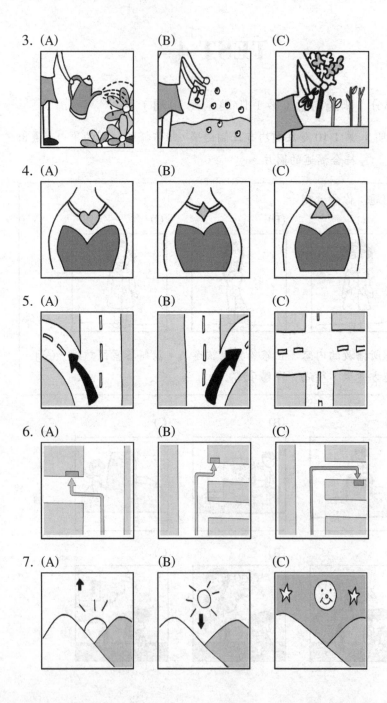

8. (A)　　　　(B)　　　　(C)

9. (A)　　　　(B)　　　　(C)

10. (A)　　　　(B)　　　　(C)

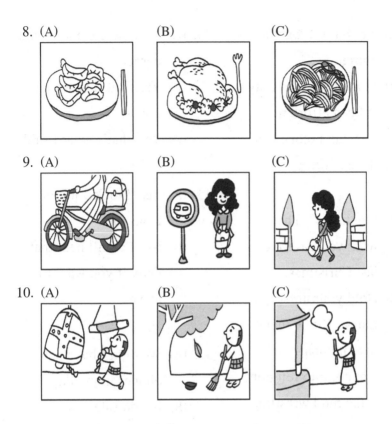

第二部分：基本問答（第 11-20 題，共 10 題）

作答說明： 第 11-20 題每題均有三個選項，請依據所聽到的對話問句，選出一個最適合的回答。

示例題：你會看到

(A) She is talking to the teacher.

(B) She is a student in my class.

(C) She is wearing a beautiful dress.

依據所播放的內容，正確答案應該選 B，請將答案紙該題「Ⓑ」的地方塗黑、塗滿，即 Ⓐ●Ⓒ。

---

11. (A) No, but I did get a
        haircut.
    (B) Sometimes, but only
        if I can afford it.
    (C) Yes, but no one has
        the answer.

12. (A) Stockings? That's
        what you gave me
        last Christmas.
    (B) Hold your horses,
        Larry. I'll be there
        in a moment.
    (C) I'm not into religion.
        I like mud wrestling.

13. (A) Bob Dylan. He's
        awful.
    (B) Long Island. It's
        about an hour east
        of Manhattan.
    (C) The Mets. I only
        cheer for losers.

14. (A) Yes, there's one on the
        corner.
    (B) Yes, you'd be a fool
        not to.
    (C) Yes, that's what I said.

15. (A) Yes, I took a job in
        Houston.
    (B) No, I didn't hear that.
    (C) Only if you want to
        leave.

16. (A) We didn't have cell
        phones in my day.
    (B) It's on sale.
    (C) Sometime tomorrow.

17. (A) Expect nothing; never
        be disappointed.
    (B) Not yet. It should be
        here any minute.
    (C) I don't know anything
        about body waxing.

18. (A) No chance. He can take care of it himself.
    (B) Again! I thought you fixed it already.
    (C) That's a good idea. I bet she could use some help.

19. (A) His girlfriend broke up with him.
    (B) His girlfriend loves her cat.
    (C) His girlfriend made up with him.

20. (A) They're lying to us.
    (B) The egg came first.
    (C) I'm going with the fish.

第三部分：言談理解（第 21-30 題，共 10 題）

作答說明： 第 21-30 題每題均有三個選項，請依據所聽到的對話或短文內容，選出一個最適合的答案。

示例題：你會看到

(A) 9:50.　　(B) 10:00.　　(C) 10:10.

依據所播放的內容，正確答案應該選 B，請將答案紙該題「Ⓑ」的地方塗黑、塗滿，即Ⓐ●Ⓒ。

---

21. (A) Distrustful.
    (B) Indifferent.
    (C) Complacent.

22. (A) Try on the sweater.
    (B) Buy the sweater.
    (C) Continue his shopping.

23. (A) Very often.
    (B) Occasionally.
    (C) Seldom.

24. (A) She washed the dishes.
    (B) She watched two hours of television.
    (C) She played computer games.

25. (A) Ms. Campbell looks much older than she is.
    (B) Ms. Campbell looks much younger than she is.
    (C) Ms. Campbell looks her age.

26. (A) Siblings.
    (B) Co-workers.
    (C) Classmates.

27. (A) Restore the Internet connection.
    (B) Resolve a customer complaint.
    (C) Receive professional help.

28. (A) Jealous.
    (B) Outraged.
    (C) Hurt.

29. (A) Finish her homework.
    (B) Visit a friend.
    (C) Speak with her grandmother.

30. (A) He has a serious illness.
    (B) He has an eating disorder.
    (C) He has rotten teeth.

TEST 4 詳解

第一部分：辨識句意

1. (**B**) (A)  (B)  (C)

Ricky is the runner-up. 瑞奇是亞軍。

* runner-up〔͵rʌnə′ʌp〕 *n.* 亞軍

2. (**A**) (A)  (B)  (C)

Daniel is worried about money. 丹尼爾擔心錢。

* worried〔′wɜɪd〕 *adj.* 擔心的 < *about* >

3. (**B**) (A)  (B)  (C)

Sally is planting seeds in her garden. 莎莉在她的花園播種。

* plant〔plænt〕 *v.* 撒（種）；播（種）　　seed〔sid〕 *n.* 種子
  garden〔′gɑrdn̩〕 *n.* 花園

4. (**A**) (A)   (B)   (C)

  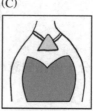

Olga's necklace has a heart-shaped pendant.

歐嘉的項鍊有一個心形的垂飾。

* necklace〔'nɛklɪs〕*n.* 項鍊   ***heart-shaped*** *adj.* 心形的
  pendant〔'pɛndənt〕*n.* 垂飾

5. (**C**) (A)   (B)   (C)

  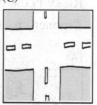

We are approaching a four-way intersection.

我們要快到一個四路交叉的路口。

* approach〔ə'protʃ〕*v.* 接近；靠近
  four-way *adj.* 四路交接的；四個方向的
  intersection〔ˌɪntə'sɛkʃən〕*n.* 十字路口

6. (**B**) (A)   (B)   (C)

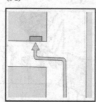 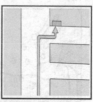 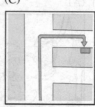

Turn right on Main Street, and it's the first house on the
left. 在主街右轉，就在左邊的第一間房子。

* main〔men〕*adj.* 主要的   ***on the left*** 在左邊

7. (**A**) (A)　　　　　(B)　　　　　(C)

  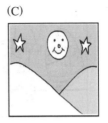

It's seven o'clock in the morning.

現在是早上七點鐘。

* o'clock〔ə'klɑk〕*adv.* …點鐘

8. (**B**) (A)　　　　　(B)　　　　　(C)

We're having chicken for dinner.

晚餐我們吃雞肉。

* have〔hæv〕*v.* 吃　　chicken〔'tʃɪkɪn〕*n.* 雞;雞肉

9. (**B**) (A)　　　　　(B)　　　　　(C)

Joan is waiting for the bus.　瓊安在等公車。

* wait〔wet〕*v.* 等待 *<for>*

10. (**B**) (A)   (B)   (C)

Thomas is raking leaves. 湯瑪士在耙葉子。

* rake〔rek〕*v.* 耙

第二部分：基本問答

11. (**A**) You look different. Are those new eyeglasses?
你看起來不一樣。那是新的眼鏡嗎？

(A) No, but I did get a haircut. 不，但我剪了頭髮。

(B) Sometimes, but only if I can afford it.
有時候，只要我負擔得起的話。

(C) Yes, but no one has the answer. 是，但沒有人有答案。

* look〔luk〕*v.* 看起來
different ('dɪfərənt)*adj.* 不一樣的；不同的
eyeglasses ('aɪ,glæsɪz)*n. pl.* 眼鏡
do + *V.* 真的～；的確～   haircut ('hɛr,kʌt)*n.* 理髮
only if 只要   afford〔ə'ford〕*v.* 負擔得起

12. (**B**) Hurry up, Martha. We're going to be late for church.
快一點，瑪莎。我們做禮拜要遲到了。

(A) Stockings? That's what you gave me last Christmas.
長襪？那是你去年聖誕節給我的。

(B) Hold your horses, Larry. I'll be there in a moment.
等一下，賴瑞。我馬上就到。

(C) I'm not into religion. I like mud wrestling.
我沒那麼熱中於宗教。我喜歡泥漿摔角。

* ***hurry up*** 趕快 　　church〔tʃɜtʃ〕*n.* 教堂；禮拜
stockings〔'stɑkɪŋz〕*n. pl.* 長襪
Christmas〔'krɪsməs〕*n.* 聖誕節 　　horse〔hɔrs〕*n.* 馬
hold *one's* ***horses*** 別著急；等一下
moment〔'momənt〕*n.* 片刻；一會兒
in a moment 馬上；立刻 　　into〔'ɪntə〕*prep.* 熱中於；關心
religion〔rɪ'lɪdʒən〕*n.* 宗教 　　mud〔mʌd〕*n.* 泥；泥漿
wrestling〔'rɛslɪŋ〕*n.* 摔角；格鬥

13. (**B**) What part of New York are you from? 你來自紐約哪裡？

　　(A) Bob Dylan. He's awful. 鮑伯狄倫。他很糟糕。

　　(B) Long Island. It's about an hour east of Manhattan.
　　　　長島。大約是曼哈頓東邊一小時的車程。

　　(C) The Mets. I only cheer for losers.
　　　　紐約大都會隊。我只替輸家歡呼。

　　* ***New York***〔nju'jɔrk〕紐約
　　Bob Dylan 鮑伯狄倫【美國民謠歌手】
　　awful〔'ɔfʊl〕*adj.* 很糟的
　　Long Island 長島【美國紐約灣的一個島】
　　east〔ist〕*adv.* 在東方
　　an hour east of… 在…東邊一小時的車程
　　Manhattan〔mæn'hætn̩〕*n.* 曼哈頓區【位於美國紐約市裡】
　　The Mets 紐約大都會 (= *The New York Mets*)【美國職業棒
　　球隊】 　　cheer〔tʃɪr〕*v.* 歡呼；喝采

14. (**A**) What's that wonderful smell? Is there a bakery nearby?
　　　　那麼香的味道是什麼？附近有麵包店嗎？

　　(A) Yes, there's one on the corner. 是的，轉角有一間。

　　(B) Yes, you'd be a fool not to.
　　　　是的，你不這麼做真是個傻子。

　　(C) Yes, that's what I said. 是的，那就是我剛才說的。

　　* wonderful〔'wʌndɚfəl〕*adj.* 極好的 　　smell〔smɛl〕*n.* 氣味
　　bakery〔'bekərɪ〕*n.* 麵包店 　　nearby〔'nɪr,baɪ〕*adv.* 在附近
　　corner〔'kɔrnɚ〕*n.* 角落；轉角 　　fool〔ful〕*n.* 傻子

15. (**A**) I hear you're leaving us, Jerry. 我聽說你要離開我們了，傑瑞。

    (A) Yes, I took a job in Houston.

       是的，我在休士頓找到工作。

    (B) No, I didn't hear that. 不，我沒有聽到。

    (C) Only if you want to leave. 只有在你想離開的時候。

    * job〔dʒɑb〕*n.* 工作

      Houston〔'hjustən〕*n.* 休士頓【美國德州工業城市】

      only if 只要；只有   leave〔liv〕*v.* 離開

16. (**C**) When do you expect to have the report finished?

    你預期何時要完成報告？

    (A) We didn't have cell phones in my day.

       在我那個時代沒有手機。

    (B) It's on sale. 這在特價。

    (C) Sometime tomorrow. 明天某個時候。

    * expect〔ɪk'spɛkt〕*v.* 期待；預期   have〔hæv〕*v.* 使⋯

      cell phone 手機   day〔de〕*n.* 時候；時代

      in *one's* ***day*** 在某人那個時代   ***on sale*** 特價

      sometime〔'sʌm,taɪm〕*adv.* 某時

17. (**B**) Did the mail arrive yet? I'm expecting a package.

    郵件到了嗎？我在等個包裹。

    (A) Expect nothing; never be disappointed.

       沒有期待，就絕不會失望。

    (B) Not yet. It should be here any minute.

       還沒。應該很快就到了。

    (C) I don't know anything about body waxing.

       我完全不知道什麼是身體除毛。

    * mail〔mel〕*n.* 郵件   expect〔ɪk'spɛkt〕*v.* 預期；等待

      package〔'pækɪdʒ〕*n.* 包裹

      disappointed〔,dɪsə'pɔɪntɪd〕*adj.* 失望的

      not yet 尚未；還沒   ***any minute*** 隨時；很快（= *very soon*）

      wax〔wæks〕*v.* 在⋯上塗蠟；打蠟於

      body waxing 身體除毛【以蠟清除身體各部位不需要的毛髮】

18. (**C**) It looks like that old lady's car has a flat tire. Let's stop and help her.

看起來好像那位老太太的車爆胎了。我們停下來幫她吧。

(A) No chance. He can take care of it himself.

不可能。他可以自己處理。

(B) Again! I thought you fixed it already.

又來了！我以為你已經修好了。

(C) That's a good idea. I bet she could use some help.

那是個好主意。我敢說她急需一些幫助。

* ***it looks like*** ~ 看似 ~ (= *it seems likely that*)
  flat〔flæt〕*adj.* 扁平的；洩氣的　　tire〔taɪr〕*n.* 輪胎
  No chance. 不可能；作夢。　　***take care of*** 照顧；處理
  fix〔fɪks〕*v.* 修理　　already〔ɔl'rɛdɪ〕*adv.* 已經
  bet〔bɛt〕*v.* 打賭；確信
  could use 很想要 (= *need sth. vey much*)

19. (**A**) What's wrong with Derek? Has he been crying?

德瑞克怎麼了？他一直在哭？

(A) His girlfriend broke up with him. 他女朋友跟他分手。

(B) His girlfriend loves her cat. 他女朋友喜歡她的貓。

(C) His girlfriend made up with him. 他女朋友跟他和好。

* ***What's wrong with*** ~? ~怎麼了？
  break up 分手　　***make up*** 和好

20. (**C**) What are you going to have? The fish or the chicken?

你要吃什麼？魚還是雞肉？

(A) They're lying to us. 他們在對我們說謊。

(B) The egg came first. 蛋先來。

(C) I'm going with the fish. 我選魚。

* lie〔laɪ〕*v.* 說謊【lie-lied-lied-lying】
  go with 選擇 (= *choose*)

第三部分：言談理解

21. (**A**) W：What was Donna doing over here? Causing more trouble?

女：多娜在這裡做什麼？製造更多麻煩嗎？

M：She was just telling me about the fight in Mr. Mason's history class.

男：她只是要告訴我關於梅森先生歷史課上打鬥的事情。

W：How would she know about it? She's not in Mason's class.

女：她怎麼會知道這件事？她沒有上梅森的課。

Question：How does the woman feel about Donna?

　　　　女士對多娜的感想是什麼？

(A) Distrustful. 不信任的。

(B) Indifferent. 不關心的。

(C) Complacent. 自滿的。

* cause〔kɔz〕v. 造成　　fight〔faɪt〕n. 打鬥
  history〔'hɪstərɪ〕n. 歷史　　class〔klæs〕n. 課
  distrustful〔dɪs'trʌstfəl〕adj. 不信任的
  indifferent〔ɪn'dɪfərənt〕adj. 漠不關心的
  complacent〔kəm'plesn̩t〕adj. 自滿的

22. (**C**) M：This is a cool sweater. How much is it?

男：這是件很酷的毛衣。多少錢？

W：It's on sale today for five-seventy-five. Tax not included.

女：今天特價 575 元。不含稅。

M：Five hundred and seventy five dollars? I'll keep looking, thanks.

男：五百七十五元？我再看看，謝謝。

Question : What will the man do next?

男士接下來會做什麼?

(A) Try on the sweater. 試穿毛衣。

(B) Buy the sweater. 買毛衣。

(C) Continue his shopping. 繼續購物。

* cool〔kul〕*adj.* 酷的　　 sweater〔'swɛtɚ〕*n.* 毛衣
  tax〔tæks〕*n.* 稅　　 include〔ɪn'klud〕*n.* 包含
  keep + V-ing 持續~　　***try on*** 試穿
  continue〔kən'tɪnju〕*v.* 繼續

23. (**C**)　W : I just read this terrific new book by J.K. Rowling.
　　　　　　　Do you read much?

女：我剛讀了 J.K. 羅琳這本很棒的新書。你常讀書嗎?

M : I like what I like, but I'm hardly a bookworm.
　　Maybe a book per month.

男：我忠於我所愛,但我不是個愛讀書的人。可能一個月一本。

W : Well, this new book is really something. It's even
　　better than Harry Potter.

女：嗯,這本書真的很棒。這本書甚至比哈利波特還棒。

Question : How often does the man read books?

男士多常唸書?

(A) Very often. 很常。

(B) Occasionally. 偶爾。

(C) Seldom. 很少。

* terrific〔tə'rɪfɪk〕*adj.* 很棒的;驚人的
  J. K. Rowling J.K. 羅琳【英國女作家,哈利波特作者】
  hardly〔'hardlɪ〕*adv.* 幾乎不
  bookworm〔'buk,wɝm〕*n.* 喜愛讀書的人;書呆子
  maybe〔'mebi〕*adv.* 可能;或許　　 per〔pɚ〕*prep.* 每…
  something〔'sʌmθɪŋ〕*n.* 重要的東西或人
  even〔'ivən〕*adv.* 甚至

> ***Harry Potter*** 哈利波特【英國作家 J.K.羅琳的兒童奇幻小說】
> occasionally〔ə'kɛʒənḷɪ〕*n.* 偶爾
> seldom〔'sɛldəm〕*adv.* 很少

24. (**A**) M：OK, Wendy. You can watch one hour of television
　　　　　　after you've done the dishes.
　　　男：好的，溫蒂。妳洗完碗之後可以看一小時的電視。
　　　W：It's Sammy's turn to wash the dishes. I did them last
　　　　　night.
　　　女：輪到珊咪洗碗了。我昨晚洗過了。
　　　M：Oh, you're right. Sammy, turn off the computer and
　　　　　get started on those dishes.
　　　男：噢，妳說得對。珊咪，關掉電腦，開始洗碗。
　　　Question：What did Wendy do last night?
　　　　　　　　　溫蒂昨晚做了什麼？
　　　(A) She washed the dishes. 她洗碗。
　　　(B) She watched two hours of television.
　　　　　她看了兩小時的電視。
　　　(C) She played computer games. 她玩電腦遊戲。

　　　* ***do the dishes*** 洗碗 (= *wash the dishes*)
　　　 it's one's turn 輪到某人　　***turn off*** 關掉 (電器)
　　　 get started on 開始做

25. (**B**) W：How old is Ms. Campbell?
　　　女：坎伯小姐幾歲？
　　　M：She's 55.
　　　男：她五十五歲。
　　　W：My goodness! She doesn't look a day over 40.
　　　女：我的天啊！她看起來最多四十歲。【詳見背景說明】
　　　Question：What does the woman mean?
　　　　　　　　　女士的意思是什麼？

(A) Ms. Campbell looks much older than she is.
坎伯小姐看起來比她實際上老很多。

(B) Ms. Campbell looks much younger than she is.
坎伯小姐看起來比她實際上年輕很多。

(C) Ms. Campbell looks her age.
坎伯小姐看起來和她的年齡相符。

* **My goodness!** 我的天呀！(= *My God!*)
look *one's* **age** 看起來和年齡相符

26. (**B**) M : Hi, Megan. How was your sales trip to Los Angeles?
男：嗨，梅根。妳去洛杉磯出差如何？

W : Terrible. I didn't get the Parker Stevenson account, Mr. Wang cancelled his order for the month, and the airlines lost my luggage.
女：糟透了。我沒得到帕克‧史蒂文森這位客戶，王先生取消本月的訂單，而且航空公司弄丟我的行李。

M : Ouch! Sorry to hear that. Welcome back anyway.
男：哎喲！很遺憾聽到那樣的事。無論如何，歡迎回來。

Question : What is the most likely relationship between the speakers? 說話者最可能是什麼關係？

(A) Siblings. 兄弟姊妹。

(B) Co-workers. 同事。

(C) Classmates. 同班同學。

* sales〔selz〕*adj.* 銷售的
sales trip 商務旅行；出差 (= *business trip*)
Los Angeles〔lɔs'ændʒələs〕*n.* 洛杉磯【位於美國加州西南部】
terrible〔'tɛrəbl〕*adj.* 可怕的；很糟的
account〔ə'kaunt〕*n.* 客戶 (= *client*)
cancel〔'kænsl〕*v.* 取消　　order〔'ɔrdɚ〕*n.* 訂單
airlines〔'ɛr,lainz〕*n. pl.* 航空公司
luggage〔'lʌgidʒ〕*n.* 行李
ouch〔autʃ〕*interj.* 哎喲【突然感到疼痛的聲音】

sorry〔'sɔrɪ〕*adj.* 遺憾的　　anyway〔'ɛnɪ,we〕*adv.* 無論如何
likely〔'laɪklɪ〕*adj.* 可能的
relationship（rɪ'leʃən,ʃɪp）*n.* 關係
siblings〔'sɪblɪŋz〕*n. pl.* 兄弟姊妹
co-worker（ko'wɜkə）*n.* 同事
classmate〔'klæs,met〕*n.* 同班同學

27. (**A**) M：Do you want me to call a technician, or do you think
　　　　　　　you can get us back online?

男：妳要我叫技術人員，或妳認為妳可以使我們重新連上網路？

W：Just give me one second. The network seems to be
　　　responding. If resetting the modem doesn't work,
　　　then yes, we need professional help.

女：給我一點時間。網路似乎有回應了。如果重開數據機沒用，
　　那我們就需要專業的協助。

M：OK. Just let me know how it goes.

男：好的。讓我知道進展如何。

Question：What is the woman trying to do?

　　　　　女士試著要做什麼？

(A) Restore the Internet connection. 恢復網路連結。

(B) Resolve a customer complaint. 解決顧客投訴。

(C) Receive professional help. 接受專業協助。

* technician〔tɛk'nɪʃən〕*n.* 專家；技術人員
　　get〔gɛt〕*v.* 使～　　online（,ɑn'laɪn）*adv.* 在線上；在網路上
　　second〔'sɛkənd〕*n.* 秒；片刻
　　network〔'nɛt,wɜk〕*n.* 網路　　seem〔sim〕*v.* 似乎
　　respond〔rɪ'spɑnd〕*v.* 反應；回應
　　reset〔ri'sɛt〕*v.* 重新調整；重新設定
　　modem〔'modəm〕*n.* 數據機　　work〔wɜk〕*v.* 有用
　　professional（prə'fɛʃənl）*adj.* 專業的　　go〔go〕*v.* 進展
　　restore（rɪ'stor）*v.* 使恢復
　　Internet〔'ɪntə,nɛt〕*n.* 網際網路
　　connection（kə'nɛkʃən）*n.* 連結

resolve〔rɪ'zɑlv〕v. 解決　　customer〔'kʌstəmɚ〕n. 顧客
complaint〔kəm'plent〕n. 抱怨；投訴
receive〔rɪ'siv〕v. 接受

28. (**A**)　M：What did you do over the weekend, Veronica?
　　　男：妳週末做了什麼，維若妮卡？
　　　W：David took me to Lake Tahoe. We skied during the
　　　　　day and gambled in the casinos at night.
　　　女：大衛帶我去太浩湖。我們白天滑雪，晚上在賭場賭博。
　　　M：Wow, I wish David would take me to Lake Tahoe. It
　　　　　sounds like you had a great time.
　　　男：哇，我希望大衛可以帶我去太浩湖。聽起來妳似乎玩得很愉
　　　　　快。
　　　Question：How does the man feel about Veronica's
　　　　　　　　　weekend? 男士對於維若妮卡的週末有何感想？
　　　(A) Jealous. 羨慕的。　　　　(B) Outraged. 生氣的。
　　　(C) Hurt. 受傷的。

　　* weekend〔'wik‚ɛnd〕n. 週末
　　　over the weekend 在週末期間
　　　Lake Tahoe 太浩湖【位於美國加州與內華達州之間的高山湖泊】
　　　ski〔ski〕v. 滑雪　　gamble〔'gæmbḷ〕v. 賭博
　　　casino〔kə'sino〕n. 賭場　　***it sounds like***~ 聽起來似乎~
　　　have a great time 玩得很愉快
　　　jealous〔'dʒɛləs〕adj. 羨慕的；嫉妒的
　　　outraged〔'aut‚redʒd〕adj. 憤怒的　　hurt〔hɝt〕adj. 受傷的

29. (**B**)　W：Mom, I finished my homework. Can I go to
　　　　　Sabrina's house now?
　　　女：媽，我做完功課了。我現在可以去莎伯琳娜的家嗎？
　　　W：Ask your father, Irene. I'm on the phone with
　　　　　Grandma.
　　　女：問妳父親，艾琳。我現在跟祖母在講電話。

W : Dad said I can go if it's all right with you.

女：爸爸說如果妳不介意，我就可以去。

Question : What does Irene want to do?　艾琳想做什麼？

(A) Finish her homework.　寫完功課。

(B) Visit a friend.　拜訪朋友。

(C) Speak with her grandmother.　跟她的祖母說話。

* finish 〔ˈfɪnɪʃ〕 v. 做完　　***on the phone***　電話中；講電話
grandma 〔ˈgrændɑ〕 n. 祖母；奶奶
be all right with sb.　某人不介意　　visit 〔ˈvɪzɪt〕 v. 拜訪

30. (**A**) M : Did you hear about Bruce? His doctor said he has
　　　　　　lung cancer.

男：妳有聽說布魯斯的事情嗎？他的醫生跟他說他罹患肺癌。

W : I wouldn't doubt it. The guy smokes five packs a day.

女：這我不會懷疑。他一天抽五包煙。

M : Well, now maybe he'll think about quitting.

男：嗯，現在或許他會考慮戒煙。

Question : What is Bruce's problem?　布魯斯有什麼問題？

(A) He has a serious illness.　他得了嚴重的病。

(B) He has an eating disorder.　他飲食失調。

(C) He has rotten teeth.　他有蛀牙。

* ***hear about***　聽說　　lung 〔lʌŋ〕 n. 肺
cancer 〔ˈkænsɚ〕 n. 癌症　　doubt 〔daʊt〕 v. 懷疑
guy 〔gaɪ〕 n. 人；傢伙　　smoke 〔smok〕 v. 抽煙
pack 〔pæk〕 n. 一包；一盒　　***think about***　考慮
quit 〔kwɪt〕 v. 停止；戒除　　serious 〔ˈsɪrɪəs〕 adj. 嚴重的
illness 〔ˈɪlnɪs〕 n. 疾病
disorder 〔dɪsˈɔrdɚ〕 n. 混亂；失調
rotten 〔ˈrɑtn̩〕 adj. 腐爛的；腐敗的
teeth 〔tiθ〕 n. pl. 牙齒【單數是 tooth】
rotten teeth　蛀牙（= *decayed teeth*）

TEST 5

第一部分：辨識句意（第 1-10 題，共 10 題）

作答說明： 第 1-10 題每題均有三個選項，請依據所聽到的單句，選出符合描述的圖片。

示例題：你會看到

(A)　　　　　　　(B)　　　　　　　(C)

依據所播放的內容，正確答案應該選 A，請將答案紙該題「Ⓐ」的地方塗黑、塗滿，即 ●ⒷⒸ。

---

1. (A)　　　　　　(B)　　　　　　(C)

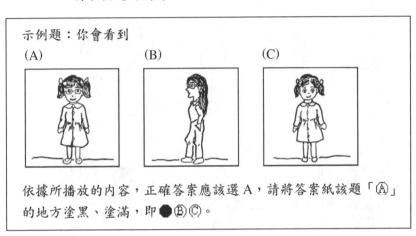

2. (A)　　　　　　(B)　　　　　　(C)

8. (A) (B) (C)

9. (A) (B) (C)

10. (A) (B) (C)

第二部分：基本問答（第 11-20 題，共 10 題）

作答說明： 第 11-20 題每題均有三個選項，請依據所聽到的對話問句，選出一個最適合的回答。

示例題：你會看到

(A) She is talking to the teacher.

(B) She is a student in my class.

(C) She is wearing a beautiful dress.

依據所播放的內容，正確答案應該選 B，請將答案紙該題「Ⓑ」的地方塗黑、塗滿，即Ⓐ●Ⓒ。

---

11. (A) You'll find out when
they move in.
(B) There is an ATM.
(C) Two million dollars.

12. (A) That's terrible. Who
would do such a thing
to you?
(B) That's wonderful.
When is the special day?
(C) That's impossible.
Where do you think
babies come from?

13. (A) No, but it's on my list
of places to visit.
(B) No, but it's a three-
legged bear.
(C) No, but it's still your
fault.

14. (A) I sure am.
(B) I sure did.
(C) I sure will.

15. (A) Sorry. I'm late for
work.
(B) Really? I thought
it was difficult.
(C) Good. I knew that
would happen.

16. (A) Close the window.
(B) Wait until he comes
back.
(C) Light some candles.

17. (A) Yes. Please sit
down.
(B) Maybe. Look at
this.
(C) Always. Take a
number.

18. (A) No way.
(B) Once in a while.
(C) What's the soup
today?

19. (A) I didn't send them. Maybe they're from your secret lover.

    (B) Add some salt. That'll make them taste better.

    (C) They're nice to look at, but honestly, they make me sneeze.

20. (A) Not very likely. You'll have to ace the final.

    (B) I thought it was poorly researched. You could have done better.

    (C) What's wrong with them?

第三部分：言談理解（第 21-30 題，共 10 題）

作答說明：第 21-30 題每題均有三個選項，請依據所聽到的對話或短文內容，選出一個最適合的答案。

示例題：你會看到

(A) 9:50.　　(B) 10:00.　　(C) 10:10.

依據所播放的內容，正確答案應該選 B，請將答案紙該題「Ⓑ」的地方塗黑、塗滿，即 Ⓐ ● Ⓒ。

---

21. (A) His age.

    (B) His height.

    (C) His name.

22. (A) Asking for directions.

    (B) Looking for a telephone.

    (C) Requesting a taxi.

23. (A) Secretary.

　　(B) Police officer.

　　(C) Salesclerk.

24. (A) A mechanic.

　　(B) A lawyer.

　　(C) A teacher.

25. (A) The man.

　　(B) The woman's brother.

　　(C) The man's father.

26. (A) Studying for an exam.

　　(B) Hiding from the woman.

　　(C) Training for an athletic event.

27. (A) He deposited money in his bank account.

　　(B) He withdrew cash from the ATM.

　　(C) He delivered the rent check to the landlord.

28. (A) Executive–secretary.

　　(B) Teacher–student.

　　(C) Coach–athlete.

29. (A) Make dinner at Bob's and rent a video.

　　(B) Go see a play and have lunch with Lucy's parents.

　　(C) Have dinner at Wally's and see a movie at the Avalon.

30. (A) A work-related task.

　　(B) A family-oriented issue.

　　(C) An upcoming holiday event.

TEST 5 詳解

第一部分：辨識句意

1. (**B**) (A)  (B) 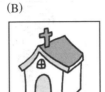 (C)

We go to church on Sundays. 我們週日上教堂。

* ***go to church*** 上教堂；做禮拜

2. (**B**) (A)  (B)  (C)

Edgar enjoys soaking in the hot springs.

艾德格喜歡泡在溫泉裡。

* ***enjoy + V-ing*** 喜歡～　　soak〔sok〕v. 浸泡

  spring〔sprɪŋ〕n. 泉　　***hot spring*** 溫泉

3. (**A**) (A)  (B)  (C)

Ivan is a heavy smoker. 伊凡是老煙槍。

* smoker〔'smokə〕n. 吸煙者
  heavy smoker 煙抽很多的人；老煙槍

4. (**C**) (A)　　　　　　(B)　　　　　　(C)

Mindy has a sore throat. 明迪喉嚨痛。

* sore〔sor〕adj. 痛的　　throat〔θrot〕n. 喉嚨

5. (**A**) (A)　　　　　　(B)　　　　　　(C)

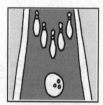  

Let's go bowling. 我們一起去打保齡球吧。

* **let's + V.** 我們一起~
  go bowling 去打保齡球

6. (**C**) (A)　　　　　　(B)　　　　　　(C)

It's Valentine's Day. 今天是情人節。

* **Valentine's Day** 情人節

7. (**B**) (A) 　　(B) 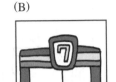　　(C)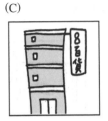

Meet me in front of the convenience store.

在便利商店前跟我見面。

* meet〔mit〕*v.* 會面　　***in front of*** 在…前面
convenience store 便利商店

8. (**A**) (A) 　　(B) 　　(C)

We had sushi for lunch. 我們午餐吃壽司。

* have〔hæv〕*v.* 吃　　sushi〔'susɪ〕*n.* 壽司【日文】
lunch〔lʌntʃ〕*n.* 午餐

9. (**C**) (A) 　　(B) 　　(C)

Tom is a veterinarian. 湯姆是位獸醫。

* veterinarian〔ˌvɛtrə'nɛrɪən〕*n.* 獸醫（= *vet*）

10. (**C**) (A)  (B) 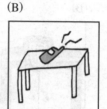 (C)

The purse is on top of the table. 皮包在桌子上。

* purse〔pɝs〕n. 皮包；錢包　　***on top of*** 在…的上面
  table〔'tebḷ〕n. 桌子；餐桌

第二部分：基本問答

11. (**A**) The Martins finally sold their house. I wonder who the new owners are.

馬丁一家終於賣了他們的房子。我想知道誰是新的主人。

(A) You'll find out when they move in.

他們搬進來後你就會知道了。

(B) There is an ATM. 那裡有台自動櫃員機。

(C) Two million dollars. 兩百萬元。

* finally〔'faɪnḷɪ〕adv. 最後；終於
  sold〔sold〕v. 賣【三態為：sell-sold-sold】
  wonder〔'wʌndɚ〕v. 想知道
  owner〔'onɚ〕n. 所有者；主人　　move〔muv〕v. 搬家
  ATM 自動櫃員機 (= *automated teller machine*)
  million〔'mɪljən〕adj. 百萬的

12. (**B**) Can you keep a secret? I'm getting married!

你可以保密嗎？我要結婚了！

(A) That's terrible. Who would do such a thing to you?

那真糟糕。誰會對你做這樣的事？

(B) That's wonderful. When is the special day?

那真太棒了。這麼特別的日子是哪一天？

(C) That's impossible. Where do you think babies come from? 那不可能。你覺得小孩哪來的？

* secret〔'sikrɪt〕*n.* 秘密　　***keep a secret*** 保密
get married 結婚　　terrible〔'tɛrəbḷ〕*adj.* 很糟的
special〔'spɛʃəl〕*adj.* 特別的
impossible〔ɪm'pɑsəbḷ〕*adj.* 不可能的

13. (**A**) Have you ever been to Taiwan? It's really a beautiful country. 你去過台灣嗎？那真的是個美麗的國家。

(A) No, but it's on my list of places to visit.

沒有，但它在我探訪地點的名單上。

(B) No, but it's a three-legged bear.

沒有，但牠是隻三隻腳的熊。

(C) No, but it's still your fault. 沒有，但這仍然是你的錯。

* ***have ever been to*** 曾經去過　　list〔lɪst〕*n.* 名單
bear〔bɛr〕*n.* 熊　　fault〔fɔlt〕*n.* 過錯

14. (**A**) Good morning! Ready for your breakfast?

早安！準備好吃早餐了嗎？

(A) I sure am. 我當然準備好了。

(B) I sure did. 我的確做了。

(C) I sure will. 我一定會的。

* ready〔'rɛdɪ〕*adj.* 準備好的　　breakfast〔'brɛkfəst〕*n.* 早餐
sure〔ʃur〕*adv.* 的確；當然

15. (**B**) The English exam was much easier than I thought it would be. 英文考試比我認為的簡單許多。

(A) Sorry. I'm late for work. 很抱歉。我上班遲到。

(B) Really? I thought it was difficult.

眞的嗎？我覺得很困難。

(C) Good. I knew that would happen.

很好。我知道那會發生。

* exam〔ɪgˈzæm〕*n.* 考試（= *examination*）
  much〔mʌtʃ〕*adv.*【強調比較級】非常；大大地
  late〔let〕*adj.* 遲到的

16. (**C**) The power went out again. What should we do?

又停電了。我們該怎麼辦？

(A) Close the window. 關窗戶。

(B) Wait until he comes back. 等到他回來。

(C) Light some candles. 點一些蠟燭。

* power〔ˈpaʊɚ〕*n.* 電力　***go out*** 熄滅；停止運轉
  window〔ˈwɪndo〕*n.* 窗戶　　light〔laɪt〕*v.* 點燃
  candle〔ˈkændl̩〕*n.* 蠟燭

17. (**A**) I got your message, Mr. Rogers. You wanted to see me?

我收到你的訊息了，羅傑斯先生。你要見我嗎？

(A) Yes. Please sit down. 是的。請坐。

(B) Maybe. Look at this. 或許。看一下這個。

(C) Always. Take a number. 總是。拿號碼牌。

* message〔ˈmɛsɪdʒ〕*n.* 訊息
  maybe〔ˈmebi〕*adv.* 可能；或許
  take a number 拿號碼牌

18. (**C**) Would you prefer soup or salad with your meal?

你比較喜歡湯還是沙拉來搭配餐點？

(A) No way. 不行。

(B) Once in a while. 偶爾。

(C) What's the soup today? 今天是什麼湯？

* prefer〔prɪˋfɝ〕*v.* 較喜歡　　soup〔sup〕*n.* 湯
salad〔ˋsæləd〕*n.* 沙拉　　meal〔mil〕*n.* 餐點
No way. 不可以；不行。
once in a while 偶爾；有時候（= *sometimes*）

19.(**C**) Look at these flowers! Aren't they beautiful?
看這些花！它們不是很美嗎？

　(A) I didn't send them. Maybe they're from your secret lover.
它們不是我送的。或許它們是你秘密愛人送的。

　(B) Add some salt. That'll make them taste better.
加些鹽。那會讓它們嚐起來更好。

　(C) They're nice to look at, but honestly, they make me sneeze.
它們看起來很棒，但是老實說，它們會讓我打噴嚏。

* send〔sɛnd〕*v.* 寄；送
secret〔ˋsikrɪt〕*adj.* 秘密的　　add〔æd〕*v.* 添加
salt〔sɔlt〕*n.* 鹽　　taste〔test〕*v.* 嚐起來
honestly〔ˋɑnɪstlɪ〕*adv.* 誠實地；老實說
sneeze〔sniz〕*v.* 打噴嚏

20.(**B**) Professor, why did you give me a C on my essay?
教授，為何我的作文你才給 C 的分數？

　(A) Not very likely. You'll have to ace the final.
不太可能。你期末考會得 A。

　(B) I thought it was poorly researched. You could have done better.
我覺得研究做得不夠。你應該可以做得更好。

　(C) What's wrong with them? 他們怎麼了？

* professor〔prə'fɛsə〕*n.* 教授
essay〔'ɛse〕*n.* 論說文；文章　　likely〔'laɪklɪ〕*adj.* 可能的
ace〔es〕*v.* 在…得到 A 的成績（= *receive a grade of A on*）
final〔'faɪnḷ〕*n.* 期末考
poorly〔'pʊrlɪ〕*adv.* 不足地；差勁地
research〔rɪ'sɜtʃ〕*v.* 研究　　***could have + p.p.*** 原本可以
What's wrong with ~? 怎麼了？

第三部分：言談理解

21. (**C**)　W：Your son is adorable. What's his name?
　　　　女：你的兒子很可愛。他叫什麼名字？
　　　　M：Thank you. His name is Henry.
　　　　男：謝謝妳。他的名字叫亨利。
　　　　W：Oh, that's my grandfather's name!
　　　　女：喔，那是我祖父的名字！
　　　　Question：What do we know about the man's son?
　　　　　　　　　關於男士的兒子我們知道什麼？
　　　　(A) His age. 他的年紀。
　　　　(B) His height. 他的身高。
　　　　(C) His name. 他的名字。

　　　　* adorable〔ə'dorəbḷ〕*adj.* 可愛的
　　　　　grandfather〔'græn,faðə〕*n.* 祖父；爺爺
　　　　　age〔edʒ〕*n.* 年齡　　height〔haɪt〕*n.* 身高

22. (**C**)　M：I need a taxi at 123 Main Street.
　　　　男：我在主街 123 號，需要一台計程車。
　　　　W：Can I get your phone number, sir?
　　　　女：先生，你的電話號碼幾號？
　　　　M：747-8343.
　　　　男：747-8343。

Question：What is the man doing? 男士在做什麼？

(A) Asking for directions. 問路。

(B) Looking for a telephone. 找電話

(C) Requesting a taxi. 叫計程車。

* taxi〔'tæksɪ〕*n.* 計程車　　main〔men〕*adj.* 主要的
phone number 電話號碼　　**ask for** 要求；請求
direction〔də'rɛkʃən〕*n.* 方向；（行路的）指引
look for 尋找　　request〔rɪ'kwɛst〕*v.* 請求；要求

23. (**C**) W：May I help you find something?

女：需要我幫你找東西嗎？

M：No, thanks. I'm just browsing.

男：不，謝謝。我只是看看。

W：Let me know if there's anything I can do.

女：如果有我可以幫忙的，請告訴我。

Question：What is the woman's job? 女士的工作是什麼？

(A) Secretary. 秘書。

(B) Police officer. 警員。

(C) Salesclerk. 售貨員。

* browse〔braʊz〕*v.* 瀏覽；隨意觀看
secretary〔'sɛkrə,tɛrɪ〕*n.* 秘書　　officer〔'ɔfəsə〕*n.* 官員
salesclerk〔'selz,klɜk〕*n.* 售貨員

24. (**A**) M：It's going to cost $500 to fix the windshield, and
another $150 for the towing service.

男：修理擋風玻璃要五百元，而且拖車服務要再付一百五十元。

W：$650! I don't have that kind of cash on me.

女：六百五十元！我沒帶那麼多現金。

M：We accept credit cards.

男：我們接受信用卡。

Question：Who is the man? 男士是誰？

(A) A mechanic. 技工。

(B) A lawyer. 律師。

(C) A teacher. 老師。

* cost〔kɔst〕*v.* 花費　　fix〔fɪks〕*v.* 修理
windshield〔'wɪnd͵ʃild〕*n.* 擋風玻璃　　tow〔to〕*v.* 拖
service〔'sɝvɪs〕*n.* 服務　　cash〔kæʃ〕*n.* 現金
credit card 信用卡　　mechanic〔mə'kænɪk〕*n.* 技工
lawyer〔'lɔjɚ〕*n.* 律師

25. (**C**) W : Is that your car? It's really cool.

女：那是你的車嗎？好酷喔。

M : Actually, it's my dad's car. He let me borrow it for
the night. Want to go for a ride?

男：事實上，是我爸的車。他讓我今晚借他的車。想要去兜風嗎？

W : Yeah! Let's go.

女：好呀！走吧。

Question：Who does the car belong to? 車子是誰的？

(A) The man. 那位男士的。

(B) The woman's brother. 那位女士的哥哥的。

(C) The man's father. 男士的父親的。

* actually〔'æktʃʊəlɪ〕*adv.* 實際上
borrow〔'baro〕*v.* 借（入）　　ride〔raɪd〕*n.* 乘車
go for a ride 開車去兜風　　belong〔bə'lɔŋ〕*v.* 屬於 *< to >*

26. (**C**) W : Hey, where have you been? It's like you fell off the
face of the earth.

女：嘿，你去哪裡了？你似乎人間蒸發了。

M : I've been training for a triathlon. If I'm not
running, I'm swimming. If I'm not swimming, I'm
on the bike.

男：我一直為了參加三項運動做訓練。如果我不跑步，我就
　　游泳。如果我不游泳，我就騎腳踏車。

W : Wow! Sounds like you have to be pretty dedicated.

女：哇！聽起來你必須非常專注。

Question : What has the man been doing?
　　　　　　男士在做些什麼？

(A) Studying for an exam. 為考試讀書。

(B) Hiding from the woman. 躲避女士。

(C) Training for an athletic event. 為運動項目做訓練。

* ***It's like~*** 似乎～；好像～ (= *It seems that~*)
fall off the face of the earth 人間蒸發 (= *disappear*
　completely) 　　　 train〔tren〕*v.* 訓練
　triathlon〔traɪˈæθlɑn〕*n.* 三項運動 (游泳、單車、賽跑)
　on the bike 騎腳踏車 　pretty〔ˈprɪtɪ〕*adv.* 非常
　dedicated〔ˈdɛdəˌketɪd〕*adj.* 專注的
　exam〔ɪgˈzæm〕*n.* 考試 (= *examination*)
　hide〔haɪd〕*v.* 躲藏　***hide from*** 躲避
　athletic〔æθˈlɛtɪk〕*adj.* 運動的
　event〔ɪˈvɛnt〕*n.* 事件；(運動) 項目

27. (**A**) W : Did you make it to the bank before it closed?

女：你有在銀行關門之前趕到嗎？

M : No, but that's OK. I was able to deposit the money
　in the ATM.

男：沒有，不過沒關係。我可以去自動櫃員機存錢。

W : That's a relief. At least now the rent check won't
　bounce.

女：真叫人鬆了一口氣。至少現在租金支票不會跳票了。

Question : What did the man do? 男士做了什麼？

(A) He deposited money in his bank account.
　他把錢存到他的銀行戶頭。

(B) He withdrew cash from the ATM.

他從自動櫃員機提現金。

(C) He delivered the rent check to the landlord.

他把租金支票送去給房東。

* ***make it to*** 趕到　　bank〔bæŋk〕*n.* 銀行

able〔'ebḷ〕*adj.* 能夠…的　　deposit〔dɪ'pazɪt〕*v.* 存（錢）

ATM 自動櫃員機（= *automated teller machine*）

relief〔rɪ'lif〕*n.* 放心；鬆了一口氣

That's a relief. 真讓人鬆了一口氣。

at least 至少　　rent〔rɛnt〕*n.* 出租；租金

check〔tʃɛk〕*n.* 支票　　bounce〔baʊns〕*v.* 遭退票；跳票

account〔ə'kaʊnt〕*n.* 帳戶

withdrew〔wɪð'dru〕*v.* 領（錢）

【三態為：withdraw-withdrew-withdrawn】

deliver〔dɪ'lɪvɚ〕*v.* 遞送　　landlord〔'lænd,lɔrd〕*n.* 房東

28.(**A**)　M：Did you have a chance to update those files?

男：妳有可能更新這些檔案嗎？

W：Yes, I did.　They're on your desk.

女：有，我做了。在你的桌上。

M：Great.　I need you to call Frank Smith and set up a meeting for Tuesday morning.

男：很好。我需要妳打電話給法蘭克‧史密斯，並安排一個週二早上的會議。

Question：What is the most likely relationship between the speakers?

講話者最可能的關係是什麼？

(A) Executive–secretary. 主管和秘書。

(B) Teacher–student. 師生。

(C) Coach–athlete. 教練和運動員。

* chance〔tʃæns〕 *n.* 機會;可能性
  update〔ʌp'det〕 *v.* 更新　　file〔faɪl〕 *n.* 檔案
  set up 安排 (= *arrange*)
  meeting〔'mitɪŋ〕 *n.* 會議
  relationship〔rɪ'leʃənˌʃɪp〕 *n.* 關係
  executive〔ɪg'zɛkjʊtɪv〕 *n.* 主管
  secretary〔'sɛkrəˌtɛrɪ〕 *n.* 秘書
  coach〔kotʃ〕 *n.* 教練　　athlete〔'æθlit〕 *n.* 運動員

29. (**C**)　M : Hey, Lucy, it's Bob. I'm calling to see if you're free tomorrow night.

男： 嘿,露西,我是鮑伯。我打電話來是要看妳明天晚上是否有空。

W : Sure, Bob. What did you have in mind?

女： 當然,鮑伯。你有什麼想法?

M : I was thinking we could have dinner at Wally's Grill and catch a late movie at the Avalon Theater.

男： 我在想我們明天可以去沃利燒烤店吃晚餐,然後再去阿瓦隆戲院看晚場電影。

Question : What will the speakers most likely do tomorrow?

說話者明天最可能做什麼?

(A) Make dinner at Bob's and rent a video.

在鮑伯家做晚餐和租影片。

(B) Go see a play and have lunch with Lucy's parents.

去看戲並和露西的父母吃午餐。

(C) Have dinner at Wally's and see a movie at the Avalon.

在沃利燒烤店吃晚餐並去阿瓦隆戲院看電影。

* free〔fri〕adj. 有空的
   have…in mind 考慮到…；意圖做…
   grill〔grɪl〕n. 烤架；燒烤店   ***catch a movie*** 看電影
   theater〔'θiətə〕n. 戲院；電影院   rent〔rɛnt〕v. 租
   video〔'vɪdɪ,o〕n. 影片   play〔ple〕n. 戲劇

30. (**C**) M：The big Halloween party is coming. Have you decided on a costume?
   男：盛大的萬聖節派對要來了。妳決定好服裝了嗎？

   W：Not yet. I haven't had time to give it much thought. How about you?
   女：還沒。我沒有時間好好想想。你呢？

   M：I'm too old for that kind of stuff.
   男：我太老了，不適合去那種場合。

   Question：What are the speakers mainly discussing?
   說話者主要在討論什麼？

   (A) A work-related task. 與工作有關的任務。
   (B) A family-oriented issue. 與家庭有關的議題。
   (C) An upcoming holiday event. 即將到來的節日活動。

* Halloween〔,hælo'in〕n. 萬聖節前夕
   party〔'pɑrtɪ〕n. 派對   ***decide on*** 決定
   costume〔'kɑstjum〕n. 服裝   ***not yet*** 尚未；還沒
   give…a thought 考慮（= think about）
   How about~? ～如何？   kind〔kaɪnd〕n. 種類
   stuff〔stʌf〕n. 東西   mainly〔'menlɪ〕adv. 主要地
   discuss〔dɪ'skʌs〕v. 討論   related〔rɪ'letɪd〕n. 有關的
   task〔tæsk〕n. 任務；工作
   oriented〔'orɪ,ɛntɪd〕adj. 以…為目標的；以…為方向的
   issue〔'ɪʃu〕n. 議題
   upcoming〔'ʌp,kʌmɪŋ〕adj. 即將來臨的
   holiday〔'hɑlə,de〕n. 節日；假日
   event〔ɪ'vɛnt〕n. 事件；大事

TEST 6

第一部分：辨識句意（第 1-10 題，共 10 題）

作答說明： 第 1-10 題每題均有三個選項，請依據所聽到的單句，選出符合描述的圖片。

示例題：你會看到

(A)   (B)   (C)

依據所播放的內容，正確答案應該選 A，請將答案紙該題「Ⓐ」的地方塗黑、塗滿，即 ●ⒷⒸ。

1. (A)   (B)   (C)

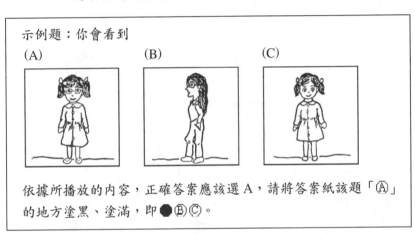

2. (A)   (B)   (C)

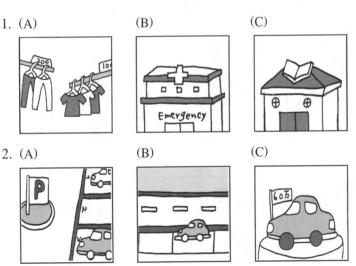

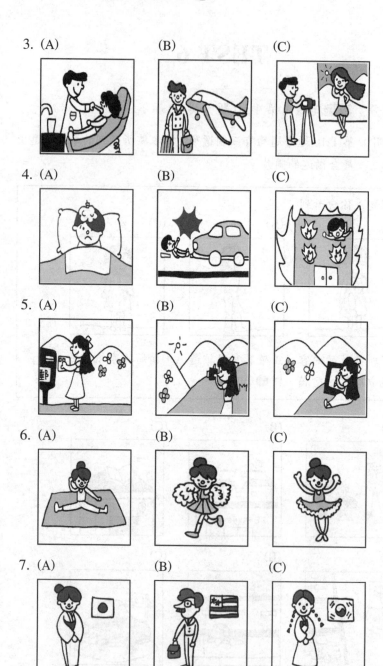

8. (A)   (B)   (C)

9. (A)   (B)   (C)

10. (A)   (B)   (C)

第二部分：基本問答（第 11-20 題，共 10 題）

作答說明： 第 11-20 題每題均有三個選項，請依據所聽到的對話問句，選出一個最適合的回答。

> 示例題：你會看到
>
> (A) She is talking to the teacher.
> (B) She is a student in my class.
> (C) She is wearing a beautiful dress.
>
> 依據所播放的內容，正確答案應該選 B，請將答案紙該題「Ⓑ」的地方塗黑、塗滿，即Ⓐ●Ⓒ。

11. (A) In this neighborhood, a one-bedroom costs five hundred dollars a month.
    (B) Most landlords post their ads on the Internet.
    (C) He doesn't get along with his roommates.

12. (A) Turn it off.
    (B) Let's order a pizza.
    (C) That's me in the corner.

13. (A) Carrots come to mind.
    (B) Quite often, actually.
    (C) It's nice. I like it.

14. (A) He said if my grades improve, he'll consider letting me go.
    (B) She said if my attitude doesn't improve, I'm due for a beating.
    (C) They said if my hearing improves, I'll be able to take regular classes.

15. (A) Sorry, I don't smoke.
    (B) Ideally, they'd stop talking.
    (C) Occasionally, she would smile and say hello.

16. (A) An exam is a type of test.
    (B) As ready as I'll ever be.
    (C) No, I haven't met Teddy.

17. (A) Interesting.
    (B) Funny.
    (C) Sunny and mild.

18. (A) I'll get right on it, sir.

(B) I'll get right over there, ma'am.

(C) I'll get right up in front, honey.

19. (A) I want a Coke.

(B) They're both equally bad.

(C) We try to avoid those places.

20. (A) Actually, none. I've never been to the northern part of my country.

(B) Are you kidding? We practically burned the place down.

(C) On Tuesdays, usually. But I don't eat beef.

第三部分：言談理解（第 21-30 題，共 10 題）

作答説明：第 21-30 題每題均有三個選項，請依據所聽到的對話或短文内容，選出一個最適合的答案。

示例題：你會看到

(A) 9:50.　　(B) 10:00.　　(C) 10:10.

依據所播放的内容，正確答案應該選 B，請將答案紙該題「Ⓑ」的地方塗黑、塗滿，即Ⓐ●Ⓒ。

21. (A) By bus and on foot.
    (B) By train and a short taxi ride.
    (C) By listening to the radio.

22. (A) They lost the game.
    (B) His exam is tomorrow.
    (C) He has an ankle injury.

23. (A) Polite.
    (B) Suffering.
    (C) Impatient.

24. (A) Brother–sister.
    (B) Cat–mouse.
    (C) Wife–husband.

25. (A) The beach.
    (B) The park.
    (C) The river.

26. (A) With cash.
    (B) With a credit card.
    (C) With a bad attitude.

27. (A) He doesn't want anyone to know that he smokes.
    (B) He used to smoke three packs a day.
    (C) He quit smoking two years ago.

28. (A) A casino in Las Vegas.
    (B) The woman's pet.
    (C) An old friend.

29. (A) She loves it.
    (B) She hates it.
    (C) She has mixed emotions.

30. (A) Thrilled.
    (B) Concerned.
    (C) Terribly busy.

TEST 6 詳解

第一部分：辨識句意

1. (**A**) (A) 　　(B) 　　(C)

Let's go shopping. 我們去購物吧。

* *let's* + *V*. 我們一起～吧
　　go shopping 去購物

2. (**B**) (A) 　　(B) 　　(C)

There is plenty of parking on the street.
街上有很多停車位。

* *plenty of* 很多　　parking〔'pɑrkɪŋ〕 *n.* 停車位

3. (**A**) (A) 　　(B) 　　(C)

Richard is a dentist. 理查是位牙醫。

　* dentist〔ˋdɛntɪst〕*n.* 牙醫

4.(**C**) (A) 　(B) 　(C)

He's trapped in a burning building. 他被困在燃燒的建築物中。

　* trap〔træp〕*v.* 使受困　　burning〔ˋbɝnɪŋ〕*adj.* 燃燒的；著火的
　building〔ˋbɪldɪŋ〕*n.* 建築物

5.(**A**) (A) 　(B) 　(C)

Kelly is mailing a letter. 凱莉在寄信。

　* mail〔mel〕*v.* 郵寄　　letter〔ˋlɛtɚ〕*n.* 信

6.(**C**) (A) 　(B) 　(C)

Judy is a ballerina. 茱蒂是位芭蕾舞女。

　* ballerina〔ˌbæləˋrinə〕*n.* 芭蕾舞女

7. (**A**) (A)   (B)   (C)

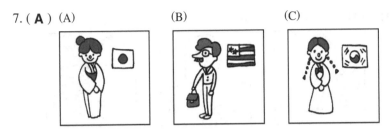

Ms. Kono is from Japan. 河野女士來自日本。

* Japan〔dʒə'pæn〕*n.* 日本

8. (**A**) (A)   (B)   (C)

I spent my summer vacation in France.

我在法國度過我的暑假。

* spent〔spɛnt〕*v.* 度過【spend 的過去式】
   summer vacation 暑假   France〔fræns〕*n.* 法國

9. (**C**) (A)   (B)   (C)

My cat loves to sleep in my lap.

我的貓喜歡在我的膝上睡覺。

* lap〔læp〕*n.* 膝上

10. (**B**) (A) 　(B) 　(C)

Henry has just enjoyed a fine meal.

亨利剛享用完一頓美好的餐點。

* enjoy〔ɪn'dʒɔɪ〕v. 享受　　meal〔mil〕n. 餐點

第二部分：基本問答

11. (**C**) Why is Mark moving out of his apartment?

為什麼馬克要搬出公寓？

(A) In this neighborhood, a one-bedroom costs five hundred dollars a month.

在這附近，一間臥室的公寓一個月要五百美元。

(B) Most landlords post their ads on the Internet.

大部分的房東會在網路上登廣告。

(C) He doesn't get along with his roommates.

他跟他的室友處得不好。

* move〔muv〕v. 搬家　　apartment〔ə'pɑrtmənt〕n. 公寓
neighborhood〔'nebə‚hud〕n. 附近地區
bedroom〔'bɛd‚rum〕n. 臥室；寢室　　cost〔kɔst〕v. 花費
landlord〔'lænd‚lɔrd〕n. 房東　　post〔post〕v. 公布；刊登

12. (**B**) I'm starving and there isn't a single thing to eat in this house. 我很餓，而房子沒有任何東西可以吃。

(A) Turn it off. 把它關掉。

(B) Let's order a pizza. 我們來點披薩吧。

(C) That's me in the corner. 角落那個人是我。

　＊ starve〔stɑrv〕*v.* 餓
　　single〔'sɪŋl〕*adj.*（與否定詞連用）連一個也沒有的
　　pull〔pʊl〕*v.* 拉；拔出　　plug〔plʌg〕*n.* 插頭
　　turn off 關掉（電器）
　　let's + V. 我們一起～吧
　　order〔'ɔrdɚ〕*v.* 訂購；點（餐）　　pizza〔'pitsə〕*n.* 披薩
　　corner〔'kɔrnɚ〕*n.* 角落；轉角

13. (**C**)　What do you think of my new hairstyle, Melvin?
　　　　你覺得我的新髮型如何，梅爾文？

　　　(A) Carrots come to mind. 我想到胡蘿蔔。

　　　(B) Quite often, actually. 事實上很常。

　　　(C) It's nice. I like it. 很不錯。我喜歡。

　　　＊ ***think of*** 認為；覺得　　hairstyle〔'hɛr,staɪl〕*n.* 髮型
　　　　carrot〔'kærət〕*n.* 胡蘿蔔　　***come to*** one's ***mind*** 某人想到
　　　　actually〔'æktʃʊəlɪ〕*adv.* 實際上

14. (**A**)　Well, what did your father say? 嗯，你父親說了什麼？

　　　(A) He said if my grades improve, he'll consider letting
　　　　　me go. 他說如果我的成績進步，他會考慮讓我去。

　　　(B) She said if my attitude doesn't improve, I'm due for
　　　　　a beating. 她說如果我的態度沒改善，我準備要挨揍。

　　　(C) They said if my hearing improves, I'll be able to take
　　　　　regular classes.
　　　　　他們說如果我的聽力進步，我就可以上一般的課程。

　　　＊ grade〔gred〕*n.* 成績　　improve〔ɪm'pruv〕*v.* 改善；進步
　　　　consider〔kən'sɪdɚ〕*v.* 考慮　　attitude〔'ætə,tjud〕*n.* 態度
　　　　due〔dju〕*adj.* 預定…的；該受…的＜*for*＞
　　　　beating〔'bitɪŋ〕*n.* 痛打　　hearing〔'hɪrɪŋ〕*n.* 聽力
　　　　take classes 上課　　regular〔'rɛgjələ〕*adj.* 普通的

15. (**A**)　Excuse me, buddy. Have you got a light?
　　　　對不起，兄弟。你有打火機嗎？

(A) Sorry, I don't smoke. 抱歉，我不抽煙。

(B) Ideally, they'd stop talking.
理想而言，他們會停止說話。

(C) Occasionally, she would smile and say hello.
她偶爾會微笑打招呼。

* **Excuse me**. 對不起。【用於引起對方注意】
buddy〔'bʌdɪ〕 *n.* 兄弟；伙伴
light〔laɪt〕 *n.* 火；打火機
smoke〔smok〕 *v.* 抽煙
ideally〔aɪ'diəlɪ〕 *adv.* 理想地；完美地
occasionally〔ə'keʒənḷɪ〕 *adv.* 偶爾；有時候
smile〔smaɪl〕 *v.* 微笑　　**say hello** 打招呼

16. (**B**) The big exam is tomorrow. Are you ready for it?
大考是明天。你準備好了嗎？

(A) An exam is a type of test. 考試是一種測試。

(B) As ready as I'll ever be. 我準備好了。

(C) No, I haven't met Teddy. 不，我還沒見到泰迪。

* exam〔ɪg'zæm〕 *n.* 考試 (= *examination*)
ready〔'rɛdɪ〕 *adj.* 準備好的　　type〔taɪp〕 *n.* 類型
As ready as I'll ever be. 我準備好了。

17. (**C**) What's the weather supposed to be like tomorrow?
明天的天氣應該會如何？

(A) Intereting. 有趣的。

(B) Funny. 好笑的。

(C) Sunny and mild. 晴朗溫暖。

* **What…is like?** …如何？
be supposed to V. 應該…
interesting〔'ɪntrɪstɪŋ〕 *adj.* 有趣的
sunny〔'sʌnɪ〕 *adj.* 晴朗的
mild〔maɪld〕 *adj.* 溫暖的

18. (**A**) Would you mind proofreading my report? I'm sure it's full of mistakes.

你會介意校對我的報告嗎？我確定裡面充滿許多錯誤。

(A) I'll get right on it, sir. 我會馬上做，長官。

(B) I'll get right over there, ma'am.
我會馬上到那裡，夫人。

(C) I'll get right up in front, honey.
我會馬上到前面，親愛的。

* mind〔maɪnd〕v. 介意　　proofread〔'pruf,rid〕v. 校對
report〔rɪ'port〕n. 報告　　sure〔sʊr〕adj. 確定的
be full of 充滿了　　mistake〔mə'stek〕n. 錯誤
get right on 馬上做 (= *do ~ immediately*)
get〔gɛt〕v. 到達　　right〔raɪt〕adv. 很快；立刻
over there 到那裡
ma'am〔mæm〕n. 太太；夫人 (= *madam*)
up〔ʌp〕adv. 向；接近　　**in front** 前面；在前方
honey〔'hʌnɪ〕n.【用於暱稱】親愛的

19. (**B**) Who is the better dancer, Reggie or Carlos?

誰比較會跳舞，雷吉還是卡洛斯？

(A) I want a Coke. 我要可口可樂。

(B) They're both equally bad. 他們一樣差。

(C) We try to avoid those places.
我們試著避開去那些地方。

* dancer〔'dænsɚ〕n. 舞者　　want〔wɑnt〕v. 想要
Coke〔kok〕n. 可口可樂
equally〔'ikwəlɪ〕adv. 同樣地
avoid〔ə'vɔɪd〕v. 避免；避開

20. (**A**) So you're from India, huh? How many times have you been to the Taj Mahal?

什麼，所以你來自印度？你去過幾次泰姬瑪哈陵？

 (A) Actually, none. I've never been to the northern part of my country.

   事實上，一次都沒有。我沒去過我們國家的北邊。

 (B) Are you kidding? We practically burned the place down. 你在開玩笑嗎？我們幾乎要把那個地方給燒毀了。

 (C) On Tuesdays, usually. But I don't eat beef.

   通常在週二。但我不吃牛肉。

* India〔ˈɪndɪə〕*n.* 印度
huh〔hʌ〕*interj.* （表示驚奇、不贊同、疑問）什麼？
time〔taɪm〕*n.* 次數 ***have been to*** 去過
Taj Mahal〔ˈtɑdʒməˈhɑl〕泰姬瑪哈陵【印度著名的白色大理石宮殿式陵墓】 actually〔ˈæktʃʊəlɪ〕*adv.* 實際上
northern〔ˈnɔrðən〕*adj.* 北部的 country〔ˈkʌntrɪ〕*n.* 國家
be kidding 開玩笑 practically〔ˈpræktɪklɪ〕*adv.* 幾乎
burn down 燒毀 beef〔bif〕*n.* 牛肉

第三部分：言談理解

21. (**A**) M：How do you get to work every day?

   男：妳每天如何去上班？

   W：I take the 96 bus to Scranton, and transfer to the 44. That takes me to Ditka Avenue and I just walk the rest of the way.

   女：我搭 96 號公車到斯克藍頓，轉 44 號公車到迪卡大道，剩下的路程用走的。

   M：Wow. Sounds like more of a journey than a commute.

   男：哇。聽起來比較像旅行而不是通勤。

   Question：How does the woman get to work every day?

      女士每天如何去上班？

   (A) By bus and on foot. 搭公車和步行。

   (B) By train and a short taxi ride. 搭火車和短程計程車。

   (C) By listening to the radio. 藉由聽廣播。

* ***get to work*** 去上班
  Scranton〔'skræntən〕n. 斯克藍頓【美國賓夕法尼亞州東北部
  的一個城市】   transfer〔træns'fɝ〕v. 換車；轉乘
  avenue〔'ævə,nju〕n. 大道   rest〔rɛst〕n. 其餘部分
  sound〔saʊnd〕v. 聽起來
  more of A ***than*** B 更像是 A 而非 B；與其說是 B 不如說是 A
  journey〔'dʒɝnɪ〕n. 旅行   commute〔kə'mjut〕n. 通勤
  on foot 步行   taxi〔'tæksɪ〕n. 計程車
  ride〔raɪd〕n. 搭乘   radio〔'rædɪ,o〕n. 無線電廣播

22. (**C**) W : How's your ankle, Jack? Will you be able to play in
   tomorrow's big game?

   女：你的腳踝怎麼了，傑克？你可以打明天重大的比賽嗎？

   M : I don't think so, Kim. The ankle is still pretty swollen.

   男：我覺得不行，金。腳踝還是很腫。

   W : That's too bad. We really need you out there.

   女：真是太可惜了。我們真的很需要你在場上。

   Question : What is wrong with the man? 男士怎麼了？

   (A) They lost the game. 他們比賽輸了。

   (B) His exam is tomorrow. 他明天要考試。

   (C) He has an ankle injury. 他的腳踝受傷。

   * ankle〔'æŋkḷ〕n. 腳踝   ***be able to V.*** 能夠～
     big〔bɪg〕adj. 重要的   pretty〔'prɪtɪ〕adv. 相當；非常
     lost〔lɔst〕v. 輸【lose 的過去式】
     That's too bad. 那真是太可惜了。
     out there 在外面；到戰場
     What's wrong with sb.? 某人怎麼了？
     exam〔ɪg'zæm〕n. 考試 (= examination)
     injury〔'ɪndʒərɪ〕n. 受傷

23. (**C**) M : How long does it take to get a cup of coffee around
   here?

   男：這裡需要多久才可以喝到咖啡？

W：Take it easy, Ralph. We just sat down.

女：放輕鬆，拉爾夫。我們才剛坐下來。

M：Aw, the service here is terrible. It's like they move in slow motion.

男：噢，這裡的服務很差。他們好像都是慢動作。

Question：Which description best matches the man?

那個描述最符合男士？

(A) Polite. 有禮貌的。　　(B) Suffering. 受苦的。

(C) Impatient. 不耐煩的。

* ***take it easy*** 放輕鬆　　service (ˈsɜvɪs) *n.* 服務
aw〔ɔ〕*interj.* （表示抗議、厭惡）噢
terrible (ˈtɛrəbḷ) *adj.* 可怕的；很糟的
It's like··· 似乎···（ = *It seems that*··· ）
move (muv) *v.* 移動；行動
motion (ˈmoʃən) *n.* 移動　　***slow motion*** 慢動作地；緩慢地
description (dɪˈskrɪpʃən) *n.* 描述
match (mætʃ) *v.* 符合　　polite (pəˈlaɪt) *adj.* 有禮貌的
suffering (ˈsʌfərɪŋ) *adj.* 受苦的
impatient (ɪmˈpeʃənt) *adj.* 不耐煩的

24.(**C**) W：Suppose I only had one leg. Would you still have married me?

女：如果我只有一條腿。你當時還會娶我嗎？

M：I'd love you even if you were missing both legs.

男：即使妳失去了兩條腿，我還是愛妳。

W：That's sweet, but it doesn't answer the question. Would you have married me?

女：你真好，但那並沒有回答問題。你當時還是會娶我嗎？

Question：What is the relationship between the speakers?

說話者的關係是什麼？

(A) Brother–sister. 兄妹。　　(B) Cat–mouse. 貓跟老鼠。

(C) Wife–husband. 夫妻。

* suppose〔sə'poz〕*conj.* 假設;如果
  marry〔'mærɪ〕*v.* 和~結婚;娶(嫁)　　***Of course.*** 當然。
  even if 即使　　miss〔mɪs〕*v.* 失去
  That's sweet (of you). 你真好。
  relationship〔rɪ'leʃən,ʃɪp〕*n.* 關係　　mouse〔maʊs〕*n.* 老鼠
  wife〔waɪf〕*n.* 妻子　　husband〔'hʌzbənd〕*n.* 丈夫

25. (**A**) M : What's the fastest way to the beach from here?

男:從這裡到海灘最快的路是什麼?

W : Well, I don't know that any one way is faster than the other.

女:嗯,我不知道哪條路比較快。

M : Thanks. You've been a lot of help.

男:謝謝。你已經幫我很多了。

Question : Where does the man want to go? 男子要去哪裡?

(A) The beach. 海灘。　　(B) The park. 公園。

(C) The river. 河流。

* beach〔bitʃ〕*n.* 海灘
  You've been a lot of help. 你已經幫了很多忙了。
  park〔pɑrk〕*n.* 公園　　river〔'rɪvɚ〕*n.* 河流

26. (**B**) W : I'm running low on cash. Do you accept credit cards?

女:我現金快要用完了。你們接受信用卡嗎?

M : Yes, we do. Your total comes to $327.85. Would you like to sign up for our member rewards program?

男:是的,我們接受。你的總金額是 327.85 元。妳要加入我們會員回饋的活動嗎?

W : No, thanks. I don't shop here often enough to make it worth my while.

女:不,謝謝。我不常來這邊購物,不值得加入。

Question : How will the woman pay for her purchase?

女士要如何支付她購買的東西?

(A) With cash. 用現金。

(B) With a credit card. 用信用卡。

(C) With a bad attitude. 用很差的態度。

* **run low on** 快用光　　cash〔kæʃ〕 n. 現金
  accept〔ək'sɛpt〕 v. 接受　　**credit card** 信用卡
  total〔'tot!〕 n. 總額　　**come to** 總計為（= amount to）
  sign〔saɪn〕 v. 簽名　　**sign up for** 同意從事；報名參加
  member〔'mɛmbɚ〕 n. 會員　　reward〔rɪ'wɔrd〕 n. 獎賞
  program〔'progræm〕 n. 計畫　　worth〔wɝθ〕 adj. 值得…的
  worth one's **while** 某人感到值得的　　**pay for** 支付
  purchase〔'pɝtʃəs〕 n. 購買（的東西）
  attitude〔'ætə,tjud〕 n. 態度

27. (**C**) M：I didn't know you smoked, Patty.

　　　　男：我不知道妳抽煙，派蒂。

　　　　W：It's my dirty little secret. Every so often I have a
　　　　　　craving for a cigarette.

　　　　女：這是我不良的小秘密。我偶爾會很想要來支煙。

　　　　M：Well, I quit about two years ago, so I know the feeling.

　　　　男：嗯，我大約兩年前戒了，所以我懂這種感覺。

　　　　Question：What is true about the man? 關於男士何者為真？

　　　　(A) He doesn't want anyone to know that he smokes.
　　　　　　他不想讓任何人知道他抽煙。

　　　　(B) He used to smoke three packs a day.
　　　　　　他以前一天抽三包煙。

　　　　(C) He quit smoking two years ago. 他兩年前戒煙。

　　　　* smoke〔smok〕 v. 抽煙
　　　　　dirty〔'dɝtɪ〕 adj. 污穢的；不正當的　　secret〔'sikrɪt〕 n. 秘密
　　　　　every so often 偶爾（= occasionally = sometimes）
　　　　　craving〔'krevɪŋ〕 n. 渴望＜for＞
　　　　　cigarette〔'sɪgə,rɛt〕 n. 香煙　　quit〔kwɪt〕 v. 停止；戒除
　　　　　used to V. 以前　　pack〔pæk〕 n. 一包；一盒

28. (**B**) W : Hey, Boris. Looking to pick up some easy cash this
weekend?

女：嘿，波里司。這週末想輕鬆賺點錢嗎？

M : You know me, Lola. I'm always interested in making
money.

男：妳知道我的，蘿拉。我一直都對賺錢很有興趣。

W : Great! I'm going to Vegas for the weekend and I
need someone to walk and feed Lucky while I'm
away. You can stay at my house.

女：不太好！我週末要去拉斯維加斯，我不在的時候，需要有
人幫我遛拉奇和餵牠。你可以住在我家。

Question : Who or what is Lucky? 拉奇是誰或是什麼東西？

(A) A casino in Las Vegas. 拉斯維加斯的一間賭場。

(B) The woman's pet. 女士的寵物。

(C) An old friend. 一位老朋友。

* look〔lʊk〕*v.* 想；期待　　***pick up*** 獲得
weekend〔'wik,ɛnd〕*n.* 週末
be interested in 對…有興趣　　***make money*** 賺錢
Vegas〔'vegəs〕*n.* 拉斯維加斯（ = *Las Vegas*）【美國內華達州的
城市，以賭場聞名】
walk〔wɔk〕*v.* 遛（狗）　　feed〔fid〕*v.* 餵
casino〔kə'sino〕*n.* 賭場　　pet〔pɛt〕*n.* 寵物

29. (**C**) M : That's very interesting. So do you enjoy working
from home?

男：那很有趣。妳喜歡在家工作嗎？

W : I do and I don't. There are pros and cons. Overall,
it's just a job.

女：喜歡也不喜歡。有好處也有壞處。整體而言，這只是個工作。

M : Yes, I say that to myself at least once a week.

男：是的，我至少每週會對自己那麼說。

Question : How does the woman feel about working from
home? 女士對於在家工作的感想如何？

(A) She loves it. 她喜歡。　　(B) She hates it. 她討厭。

(C) She has mixed emotions. 她正負面的情緒都有。

* interesting (ˈɪntrɪstɪŋ) *adj.* 有趣的　*pros and cons* 利弊
overall (ˈovə͵ɔl) *adv.* 整體來說　*at least* 至少
once (wʌns) *adv.* 一次　mixed (mɪkst) *adj.* 混合的；摻雜的
emotion (ɪˈmoʃən) *n.* 情緒；感情
mixed emotions 正面負面的情緒都有；百感交集

30. (**A**) W : I hope you don't mind, but Edward will be joining us
for dinner tonight.

女：我希望你不要介意，但是愛德華今晚會和我們一起吃晚餐。

M : Of course I don't mind. What a lovely surprise! It's
been so long since we've had him over.

男：我當然不介意。真令人驚喜！自從上次邀請他過來，已經過
很久了。

W : Yes, well, he's been terribly busy promoting his
latest book.

女：是的，嗯，他最近正忙著要推銷自己的新書。

Question : How does the man feel about Edward coming
for dinner? 男士對於愛德華來吃晚餐的感想如何？

(A) Thrilled. 非常興奮的。　　(B) Concerned. 擔心的。

(C) Terribly busy. 非常忙。

* mind (maɪnd) *v.* 介意
join (dʒɔɪn) *v.* 加入；和～一起做同樣的事
of course 當然　lovely (ˈlʌvlɪ) *adj.* 極好的
surprise (səˈpraɪz) *n.* 意外的事；驚奇
have sb. over 邀請某人來家裡作客
terribly (ˈtɛrəblɪ) *adv.* 非常地　*be busy* + *V-ing* 忙於
promote (prəˈmot) *v.* 促銷　latest (ˈletɪst) *adj.* 最新的
thrilled (θrɪld) *adj.* 興奮的
concerned (kənˈsɝnd) *adj.* 擔心的

TEST 7

第一部分：辨識句意（第 1-10 題，共 10 題）

作答說明： 第 1-10 題每題均有三個選項，請依據所聽到的單句，選出符合描述的圖片。

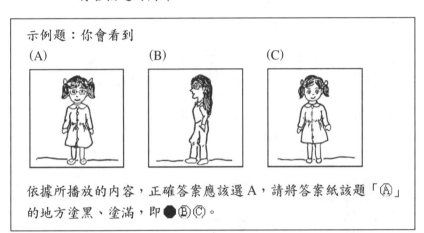

示例題：你會看到

(A)　　　　　(B)　　　　　(C)

依據所播放的內容，正確答案應該選 A，請將答案紙該題「Ⓐ」的地方塗黑、塗滿，即 ●ⒷⒸ。

1. (A)　　　　　(B)　　　　　(C)

2. (A)　　　　　(B)　　　　　(C)

8. (A)　　(B)　　(C)

9. (A)　　(B)　　(C)

10. (A)　　(B)　　(C)

第二部分：基本問答（第 11-20 題，共 10 題）

作答說明：　第 11-20 題每題均有三個選項，請依據所聽到的對話問
　　　　　　句，選出一個最適合的回答。

示例題：你會看到

(A) She is talking to the teacher.

(B) She is a student in my class.

(C) She is wearing a beautiful dress.

依據所播放的內容，正確答案應該選 B，請將答案紙該題「Ⓑ」
的地方塗黑、塗滿，即Ⓐ●Ⓒ。

---

11. (A) Wanda's not sick.
    (B) I'll make Wanda upset.
    (C) Not yet, Wanda.

12. (A) Really? You look fine to me.
    (B) Seriously? That's pretty heavy stuff.
    (C) Are you sure? Check again.

13. (A) David Beckham and Posh Spice.
    (B) Biscuits and gravy.
    (C) Just a bit of sugar; hold the cream.

14. (A) Sure. It would look good on you.
    (B) Almost. Until it went on sale.
    (C) Rats! She's a size 12.

15. (A) Yes, I would.
    (B) Stop! That hurts.
    (C) No, it's yours.

16. (A) All accounted for, Ms. Brown.
    (B) It was like that when I got here, Ms. Smith.
    (C) None so far, Ms. White.

17. (A) Send the dish back to the kitchen.
    (B) Use exact change when boarding the bus.
    (C) Push the button and wait.

18. (A) It's summer in Paris.
    (B) I would agree.
    (C) The Eiffel Tower.

19. (A) That's a good idea.
    (B) This is a fact of life.
    (C) They are uneducated.

20. (A) You'll be sorry.
    (B) You'd be much better off.
    (C) You're very welcome.

第三部分：言談理解（第 21-30 題，共 10 題）

作答說明：第 21-30 題每題均有三個選項，請依據所聽到的對話或短文內容，選出一個最適合的答案。

> 示例題：你會看到
>
> (A) 9:50.　　(B) 10:00.　　(C) 10:10.
>
> 依據所播放的內容，正確答案應該選 B，請將答案紙該題「Ⓑ」的地方塗黑、塗滿，即Ⓐ●Ⓒ。

21. (A) For Carol.
    (B) In Miami.
    (C) Next Sunday.

22. (A) Their friend.
    (B) Their daughter.
    (C) Their son.

23. (A) Printer ink.
    (B) School supplies.
    (C) Breakfast.

24. (A) In a bakery.
    (B) In an airport.
    (C) In a supermarket.

25. (A) He isn't qualified
       for the promotion.
    (B) He isn't strong
       enough to lift the
       desk.
    (C) He isn't friendly with
       his colleagues.

26. (A) It's justified.
    (B) It's a little more than
       she expected.
    (C) It's unfair.

27. (A) A contest.
    (B) A very intelligent
       insect.
    (C) A skinny fashion
       model.

28. (A) She is French.
    (B) She is in pain.
    (C) She is watching her
       weight.

29. (A) Wait twenty-four
       hours.
    (B) See the doctor.
    (C) Have her house
       sprayed for bugs.

30. (A) He went to band
       practice.
    (B) He went on a safari.
    (C) He went to a concert.

TEST 7 詳解

第一部分：辨識句意

1. (**C**) (A) (B) (C)

Toby is having a picnic. 托比正在野餐。

* picnic〔'pɪknɪk〕n. 野餐

2. (**C**) (A) (B) (C)

Kirby won the competition. 柯比贏得比賽。

* won〔wʌn〕v. 贏得【三態為：win-won-won】
competition〔ˌkɑmpə'tɪʃən〕n. 比賽

3. (**A**) (A) (B) (C)

Henry would like an egg sandwich. 亨利想要吃三明治夾蛋。

* **would like** 想要　　sandwich〔'sændwɪtʃ〕 n. 三明治

4. (**C**) (A)　　　　　　(B)　　　　　　(C)

Would you care for a cup of tea? 你想要一杯茶嗎？

* **care for** 想要　　tea〔ti〕 n. 茶

5. (**B**) (A)　　　　　　(B)　　　　　　(C)

Greg likes to work by candlelight.

格雷格喜歡在燭光下工作。

* candlelight〔'kændl̩ˌlaɪt〕 n. 燭光　　**by candlelight** 在燭光下

6. (**B**) (A)　　　　　　(B)　　　　　　(C)

Jack is a talented basketball player.

傑克是個有天分的籃球選手。

* talented〔ˋtæləntɪd〕adj. 有天分的
basketball〔ˋbæskɪt͵bɔl〕n. 籃球
player〔ˋpleɚ〕n. 運動員；選手

7. (**A**) (A)　　　　　(B)　　　　　(C)

Iris has books in her backpack. 愛麗絲背包裡放著書。

　* backpack〔ˋbæk͵pæk〕n. 背包

8. (**A**) (A)　　　　　(B)　　　　　(C)

It's Halloween. 這是萬聖節前夕。

　* Halloween〔͵hæləˋin〕n. 萬聖節前夕

9. (**B**) (A)　　　　　(B)　　　　　(C)

Rudy is very happy. 露迪很高興。

　* happy〔ˋhæpɪ〕adj. 高興的

10. (**A**) (A)   (B)   (C)

My grandfather owns a farm. 我祖父有農場。

* grandfather〔'græn,faðɚ〕*n.* 祖父;爺爺
own〔on〕*v.* 擁有   farm〔farm〕*n.* 農場

第二部分:基本問答

11. (**C**) Phil, it's Wanda. Did you get a chance to look over the
files I sent? 菲爾,我是汪達。你有看一下我寄過去的檔案嗎?

(A) Wanda's not sick. 汪達沒有生病。

(B) I'll make Wanda upset. 我會讓汪達不高興。

(C) Not yet, Wanda. 還沒,汪達。

* chance〔tʃæns〕*n.* 機會;可能性   ***look over*** 粗略地看
file〔faɪl〕*n.* 文件   sent〔sɛnt〕*v.* 寄;送【send 的過去式】
sick〔sɪk〕*adj.* 生病的   upset〔ʌp'sɛt〕*adj.* 不高興的
not yet 尚未;還沒

12. (**A**) The doctor said I need to lose weight.
醫生說我需要減肥。

(A) Really? You look fine to me.
真的嗎?對我來說你看起來很好。

(B) Seriously? That's pretty heavy stuff.
認真的嗎?那是很重的東西。

(C) Are you sure? Check again.
你確定嗎?再檢查一次。

* weight〔wet〕*n.* 重量；體重　　*lose weight* 減重
look〔lʊk〕*v.* 看起來
seriously〔'sɪrɪəslɪ〕*adv.* 嚴肅地；認真地
pretty〔'prɪtɪ〕*adv.* 非常；相當　　heavy〔'hɛvɪ〕*adj.* 重的
stuff〔stʌf〕*n.* 東西　　sure〔ʃʊr〕*adj.* 確定的
check〔tʃɛk〕*v.* 檢查

13. (**C**) How do you take your coffee?　你喝怎樣的咖啡？

　　(A) David Beckham and Posh Spice.
　　　　大衛‧貝克漢和時髦辣妹。

　　(B) Biscuits and gravy.　肉汁小餅。

　　(C) Just a bit of sugar; hold the cream.
　　　　只要一點糖，不要奶精。【詳見背景說明】

　　* take〔tek〕*v.* 吃；喝
　　David Beckham 大衛‧貝克漢【英國足球明星】
　　posh〔pɑʃ〕*adj.* 時髦的　　spice〔spaɪs〕*n.* 香料；調味品
　　Posh Spice 時髦辣妹【貝克漢的妻子，原名維多利亞】
　　biscuit〔'bɪskɪt〕*n.* 餅乾　　gravy〔'grevɪ〕*n.* 肉汁
　　biscuits and gravy 肉汁小餅【一種美式早餐】
　　a bit of 一點點　　sugar〔'ʃʊgɚ〕*n.* 糖
　　hold〔hold〕*v.* 保留；不給　　cream〔krim〕*n.* 奶精

14. (**A**) Look! This dress is on sale. Should I buy it?
　　你看！這洋裝在特價。我該買嗎？

　　(A) Sure. It would look good on you.
　　　　當然。這件妳穿起來會很好看。

　　(B) Almost. Until it went on sale.
　　　　幾乎。直到它特價。

　　(C) Rats! She's a size 12.　我不相信！她穿 12 號。

　　* dress〔drɛs〕*n.* 洋裝　　*on sale* 特價中
　　look good on sb. （衣服）適合某人
　　Rats! 【表示不信、失望等】我不相信！

15. (**A**) I'm sorry you were unhappy with our service, ma'am.
Would you like to speak with a manager?
很抱歉妳對我們的服務感到不滿意，太太。妳想要和我們的經
理談談嗎？

　(A) Yes, I would. 是的，我要。

　(B) Stop! That hurts. 快停下來！會痛。

　(C) No, it's yours. 不，那是你的。

　* **be unhappy with** 對…感到不滿意
　　service〔ˋsɝvɪs〕*n.* 服務
　　ma'am〔mæm〕*n.* 太太；小姐（= *madam* ）
　　would like to V. 想要～　　manager〔ˋmænɪdʒɚ〕*n.* 經理
　　hurt〔hɝt〕*v.* 疼痛

16. (**C**) Good morning, Peter. Do I have any messages?
早安，彼得。我有任何留言嗎？

　(A) All accounted for, Ms. Brown.
　　所有人都在場，布朗小姐。

　(B) It was like that when I got here, Ms. Smith.
　　當我到這裡的時候，就像那樣，史密斯小姐。

　(C) None so far, Ms. White.
　　目前沒有，懷特小姐。

　* message〔ˋmɛsɪdʒ〕*n.* 留言
　　account for 說明；知道…的下落
　　all accounted for 所有人都在場（= *all people are present* ）
　　get〔gɛt〕*v.* 到達　　**so far** 到目前爲止

17. (**A**) My steak is over-cooked and the potatoes are cold.
我的牛排煮太老，而且馬鈴薯是冷的。

　(A) Send the dish back to the kitchen. 把餐點送回廚房。

　(B) Use exact change when boarding the bus.
　　搭公車的時候，要用剛好的零錢。

　(C) Push the button and wait. 按按鈕然後等待。

* steak〔stek〕*n.* 牛排
over-cook〔͵ovə'kʊk〕*v.* 把…煮過熟；把…煮老
potato〔pə'teto〕*n.* 馬鈴薯
dish〔dɪʃ〕*n.* 菜餚　　kitchen〔'kɪtʃɪn〕*n.* 廚房
exact〔ɪg'zækt〕*adj.* 準確的；恰好的
change〔tʃendʒ〕*n.* 零錢
board〔bord〕*v.* 上（船、飛機）　　push〔pʊʃ〕*v.* 推；按
button〔'bʌtn̩〕*n.* 按鈕

18. (**B**) So you've been to Paris? They say it's best to go in the spring. 所以你去過巴黎？聽說春天去最好。

　(A) It's summer in Paris. 巴黎現在是夏天。

　(B) I would agree. 我會同意。

　(C) The Eiffel Tower. 艾菲爾鐵塔。

* ***have been to*** 去過～
Paris〔'pærɪs〕*n.* 巴黎【法國首都】
spring〔sprɪŋ〕*n.* 春天　　summer〔'sʌmɚ〕*n.* 夏天
agree〔ə'gri〕*v.* 同意
Eiffel Tower〔'aɪfl̩'taʊɚ〕艾菲爾鐵塔【巴黎最具代表性的一座建築物】

19. (**A**) Traffic is awful this afternoon. We'd better leave a bit earlier than planned.
今天下午的交通很糟。我們最好比原訂計畫早一點離開。

　(A) That's a good idea. 好主意。

　(B) This is a fact of life. 這就是現實。

　(C) They are uneducated. 他們沒受過教育。

* traffic〔'træfɪk〕*n.* 交通
awful〔'ɔfʊl〕*adj.* 可怕的；很糟的　　***had better V.*** 最好～
a bit 稍微；一點　　plan〔plæn〕*v.* 計畫
fact〔fækt〕*n.* 事實　　***a fact of life*** 現實；殘酷的事實
uneducated〔ʌn'ɛdʒə͵ketɪd〕*adj.* 未受教育的

20. (**C**) Thanks for helping me with the essay. I couldn't have done it without you.

謝謝你幫我寫這篇文章。沒有你，我無法完成。

(A) You'll be sorry. 你會後悔的。

(B) You'd be much better off. 你會更富裕許多。

(C) You're very welcome. 不客氣。

* ***help*** *sb.* ***with*** *sth.* 幫助某人做某事
   essay (ˈɛse) *n.* 論說文；文章
   couldn't have + *p.p.* 原本無法~
   sorry (ˈsɔrɪ) *adj.* 抱歉的；後悔的
   much (mʌtʃ) *adv.* 【加強比較級】更加
   better off 更富裕；情況更好【原級為 well off (富裕的)】

第三部分：言談理解

21. (**C**) M : Hi, Carol. I'm throwing a dinner party next Sunday and I'd be honored if you could make it.

男：嗨，卡蘿。我下週日正要舉辦一個晚宴，如果妳能來，我會感到很榮幸。

W : That's very nice of you, Hugo, but I'm afraid I'll be in Miami next Sunday.

女：你人真好，雨果，但我下週日恐怕會在邁阿密。

M : Oh, that's a shame. Maybe next time?

男：喔，真可惜。或許下一次吧？

Question : When will the man's dinner party be held?

男士何時要舉辦他的晚宴？

(A) For Carol. 為了卡蘿。

(B) In Miami. 在邁阿密。

(C) Next Sunday. 下週日。

* ***throw a party*** 舉辦派對（ = *have a party*）
honored〔'ɑnəd〕*adj.* 感到光榮的　***make it*** 能來
Miami〔maɪ'æmɪ〕*n.* 邁阿密【美國佛羅里達州東南部濱海的城市】
shame〔ʃem〕*n.* 可惜的事
maybe〔'mebɪ〕*adv.* 可能；或許
held〔hɛld〕*v.* 舉辦【三態為：hold-held-held】

22. (**C**) W : Have you given any thought to our discussion last
night?

女：你有考慮一下我們昨晚討論的事情嗎？

M : Yes, and I think we should let Jimmy go on the trip.
It will be good for him. We need to encourage his
independence.

男：有，而我覺得我們應該讓吉米去旅行。這對他很好。我們
需要鼓勵他獨立。

W : You're right. But I won't stop worrying about him
until he comes home in one piece.

女：你說得對。但在他安然無恙回到家之前，我無法不擔心他。

Question : Who is Jimmy in relation to the speakers?
吉米跟說話者是什麼關係？

(A) Their friend. 他們的朋友。

(B) Their daughter. 他們的女兒。

(C) Their son. 他們的兒子。

* ***give thought to*** 考慮（ = *think about*）
discussion〔dɪ'skʌʃən〕*n.* 討論　***go on the trip*** 去旅行
encourage〔ɪn'kɝɪdʒ〕*v.* 鼓勵
independence〔͵ɪndɪ'pɛndəns〕*n.* 獨立
You're right. 你說得對。　***stop + V-ing*** 停止～
in one piece 完整的；安然無恙的
relationship〔rɪ'leʃən͵ʃɪp〕*n.* 關係

23. (**A**) M : The printer is out of ink. Do you know where we keep the refill cartridges?

男：印表機沒墨水了。你知道我們填充墨水匣放在哪裡嗎？

W : Check the supply cabinet, Chad.

女：看一下供應櫃有沒有，查得。

M : Give me a break, Nancy. I'm new around here.

男：饒了我吧，南西。我新來的。

Question : What is the man looking for? 男士在找什麼？

(A) Printer ink. 印表機的墨水。

(B) School supplies. 文具。

(C) Breakfast. 早餐。

* printer〔'prɪntɚ〕*n.* 印表機   ink〔ɪnk〕*n.* 墨水
 out of ink 墨水沒了
 refill〔ri'fɪl〕*n.* 再裝滿；填滿的換裝物
 cartridge〔'kɑrtrɪdʒ〕*n.* 墨水匣
 refill cartridge 填充墨水匣   check〔tʃɛk〕*v.* 檢查；察看
 supply〔sə'plaɪ〕*adj.* 供應的；補給的
 cabinet〔'kæbənɪt〕*n.* 陳列櫃
 give sb. a break 饒了某人   *look for* 尋找
 supplies〔ə'plaɪz〕*n. pl.* 生活用品；補給品
 school supplies 學校用品；文具

24. (**C**) W : Excuse me, do you carry whole wheat flour?

女：很抱歉，你們有全麥麵粉？

M : If we do, it would be in aisle 3, with all the baking ingredients.

男：如果有的話，會在走道第三排，和所有烘焙原料放在一起。

W : Thanks. I'll do that.

女：謝謝。我會去看看。

Question：Where is this conversation taking place?

　　　　　這對話出現在哪裡？

(A) In a bakery. 在麵包店。

(B) In an airport. 在機場。

(C) In a supermarket. 在超市。

* carry〔'kærɪ〕*v.* 賣；出售（ = *have…for sale*）
  whole〔hol〕*adj.* 全部的　　wheat〔hwit〕*n.* 小麥
  whole wheat *adj.* 全麥的　　flour〔flaʊr〕*n.* 麵粉
  aisle〔aɪl〕*n.* 通道；走道
  baking〔'bekɪŋ〕*adj.* 烘烤的；烘焙的
  ingredient（ɪn'gridɪənt）*n.* 原料
  conversation〔ˌkɑnvə'seʃən〕*n.* 對話
  take place 發生；出現　　bakery〔'bekərɪ〕*n.* 麵包店
  airport〔'ɛrˌport〕*n.* 機場
  supermarket〔'supəˌmarkɪt〕*n.* 超級市場

25. (**A**) M : Did you hear that Andy got promoted to manager of
　　　　　　　the marketing department? Are you kidding me?

　　　男：妳聽說安迪升為行銷部門經理嗎？妳在跟我開玩笑嗎？

　　　W : I know. He's only been here six months and he
　　　　　doesn't know the first thing about marketing.

　　　女：我知道。他是才到這裡六個月，而且他完全不懂行銷。

　　　M : I give it a week before someone quits or we lose an
　　　　　important client.

　　　男：我認為不用一週就會有人辭職，不然就是我們會失去一位重
　　　　　要的客戶。

　　　Question：What do the speakers think about Andy?

　　　　　　　　說話者覺得安迪如何？

　　　(A) He isn't qualified for the promotion.
　　　　　他沒有資格升遷。

(B) He isn't strong enough to lift the desk.

他不夠強壯，無法舉起辦公桌。

(C) He isn't friendly with his colleagues.

他對他的同事不友善。

* **promote** 〔 prə'mot 〕 *v.* 使升遷

　manager 〔'mænɪdʒɚ 〕 *n.* 經理

　marketing 〔'markɪtɪŋ 〕 *n.* 行銷

　department 〔 dɪ'partmənt 〕 *n.* 部門

　Are you kidding me? 你在對我開玩笑嗎？

　not know the first thing about 完全不懂（ = *not know*
　　anything about ）

　***give sth.* + 時間**　認為某事能持續（多久）

　quit 〔 kwɪt 〕 *v.* 辭職　　**client** 〔'klaɪənt 〕 *n.* 客戶

　qualified 〔'kwalə,faɪd 〕 *adj.* 有…資格的＜*for*＞

　promotion 〔 prə'moʃən 〕 *n.* 升遷　　**lift** 〔 lɪft 〕 *v.* 舉起

　desk 〔'dɛsk 〕 *n.* 書桌；辦公桌

　friendly 〔'frɛndlɪ 〕 *adj.* 友善的

　colleague 〔'kalig 〕 *n.* 同事（ = *co-worker* ）

26. (**C**)　W：Did you see this? The cable company charged us with
　　　　　　a huge late fee on this month's bill.

　　　女：你有看到這個嗎？有線電視公司因我們這個月遲繳帳單，
　　　　　要收一筆龐大的費用。

　　　M：That's because we were late last month. If you
　　　　　recall, we were out of town and I forgot to pay the
　　　　　bill before we left.

　　　男：那是因為我們上個月遲繳。如果妳回想一下，我們到外地
　　　　　去，而我忘了在離開前繳帳單。

　　　W：That's right. But still, the fee is totally unreasonable.
　　　　　Fifty dollars? They can't do that and get away with it.

女：沒錯。但是，這費用根本不合理。五十元？他們不能那麼做
而卻沒人管。

Question：How does the woman feel about the late fee?
女士對於遲繳的費用感想如何？

(A) It's justified. 是合理的。

(B) It's a little more than she expected. 有一點超過預期。

(C) It's unfair. 不公平的。

* cable〔'kebḷ〕*n.* 電纜；有線電視
cable company 有線電視公司
charge sb. with… 使某人遭受…；跟某人索取…（錢）
huge〔hjudʒ〕*adj.* 龐大的；巨大的　　fee〔fi〕*n.* 費用
recall〔rɪ'kɔl〕*v.* 回想起　　*out of town* 出城；到外地
still〔stɪl〕*adv.* 儘管如此
bill〔bɪl〕*n.* 帳單
totally〔'totḷɪ〕*adv.* 完全地
unreasonable〔ʌn'riznəbḷ〕*adj.* 不合理的
get away with （做壞事）逃脫（懲罰）；（做某事）不用承擔
後果
justified〔'dʒʌstə‚faɪd〕*adj.* 有正當理由的
expect〔ɪk'spɛkt〕*v.* 期待；預期
unfair〔ʌn'fɛr〕*adj.* 不公平的；不當的

27. (**A**) M：How did you do in the spelling bee, Gloria?
男：妳拼字比賽結果如何，葛羅莉亞？

W：I came in third. I misspelled "anorexic."
女：我得到第三名。我拼錯了"anorexic"。

M：That's pretty good! I can't even pronounce that word
correctly, let alone spell it.
男：那很棒了！我連那個字都不會唸，更不用說拼出來了。

Question：What is a spelling bee? 什麼是 spelling bee？

(A) A contest.　一場比賽。

(B) A very intelligent insect.　一種很聰明的昆蟲。

(C) A skinny fashion model.　一位很瘦的時尚模特兒。

* spelling〔'spɛlɪŋ〕*n.* 拼字
bee〔bi〕*n.* 蜜蜂；（工作、娛樂等）聚會
spelling bee 拼字比賽　　***come in*** + 序數　得到（名次）
misspell〔mɪs'spɛl〕*v.* 拼錯
anorexic〔͵ænə'rɛksɪk〕*n.* 患厭食症的人
pronounce〔prə'naʊns〕*v.* 發音
correctly〔kə'rɛktlɪ〕*adv.* 正確地
let alone 更不用說（= *not to mention* ）
contest〔'kɑntɛst〕*n.* 比賽
intelligent〔ɪn'tɛlədʒənt〕*adj.* 聰明的
insect〔'ɪnsɛkt〕*n.* 昆蟲
skinny〔'skɪnɪ〕*adj.* 很瘦的；皮包骨
fashion〔'fæʃən〕*n.* 流行；時尚　　model〔'mɑdl̩〕*n.* 模特兒

28. (**C**) W：Are you going to finish your French fries?　If not, I'll
　　　　　 eat them.

　　女：你要把你的薯條吃光嗎？如果沒有，我要吃了。

　　M：Linda!　What about your diet?

　　男：琳達！妳不是說要節食？

　　W：I'm still on it.　A couple of French fries aren't going
　　　　to hurt.

　　女：我還在節食呀。吃一些薯條不會怎樣。

　　Question：What do we know about the woman?

　　　　　　　關於女士我們知道什麼？

　　(A) She is French.　她是法國人。

　　(B) She is in pain.　她感到痛苦。

　　(C) She is watching her weight.　她很注意她的體重。

* finish〔'fɪnɪʃ〕*v.* 吃完;喝光　　***French fries*** 薯條
diet〔'daɪət〕*n.* 節食　　***be on a diet*** 節食中
a couple of 幾個;一些　　hurt〔hɜt〕*v.* 有害;造成損失
French〔frɛntʃ〕*adj.* 法國人的　　pain〔pen〕*n.* 疼痛;痛苦
be in pain 感到痛苦　　watch〔watʃ〕*v.* 注意
weight〔wet〕*n.* 重量;體重

29. (**B**)　M：Are you going to the doctor today?

男：妳今天要去看醫生嗎?

W：No, I cancelled the appointment. I'm starting to feel
much better. It was probably one of those twenty-
four hour bugs.

女：不,我取消了預約。我開始覺得比較好了。這可能是那種
一天就能痊癒的小病。

M：I don't know. I think it's better to be safe than sorry.
I would re-schedule that appointment if I were you.

男：我不知道。我覺得要安全總比後悔好。如果我是妳,我會
再預約一次。

Question：What does the man think the woman should
do?　男士覺得女士應該怎麼做?

(A) Wait twenty-four hours. 等二十四個小時。

(B) See the doctor. 看醫生。

(C) Have her house sprayed for bugs.
給她的房子噴灑滅蟲藥。

* ***go to the doctor*** 去看醫生 (*= go to see the doctor*)
cancel〔'kænsḷ〕*n.* 取消
appointment〔ə'pɔɪntmənt〕*n.* 預約
probably〔'prɑbəblɪ〕*adv.* 可能
bug〔bʌg〕*n.* 小蟲;小毛病 (*= small illness*)

a twenty-four hour bug 二十四小時的病；一天內就痊癒的
小病 (= *an illness that lasts only one day and is not very*
serious)
better safe than sorry 安全總比後悔好
re-schedule〔 ri'skɛdʒul 〕*v.* 重新安排…的時間
spray〔 spre 〕*v.* 噴灑（農藥等）＜*for*＞

30. (**C**)　W : How was the concert last night, Allan?　I heard it was
sold out.

女：昨天的演唱會如何，艾倫？我聽說票賣光了。

M : It was incredible, Laura.　The band sounded great
and the crowd was going wild!

男：真的難以置信，蘿拉。樂團聽起來很棒，而且聽眾都爲之
瘋狂！

W : I'm so jealous.　I never get to have any fun.

女：我好羨慕你。我從沒能夠好好玩樂。

Question : What did Allan do last night?

艾倫昨晚做了什麼？

(A) He went to band practice. 他去樂團練習。

(B) He went on a safari. 他去狩獵旅行。

(C) He went to a concert. 他去聽演唱會。

* concert〔'kɑnsɝt〕*n.* 演唱會　　***sell out*** 賣光；售完
incredible〔 ɪn'krɛdəbḷ 〕*adj.* 令人無法置信的
sound〔 saund 〕*v.* 聽起來　　crowd〔 kraud 〕*n.* 群衆；大衆
go〔 go 〕*v.* 變得　　wild〔 waɪld 〕*adj.* 瘋狂的
jealous〔'dʒɛləs〕*adj.* 羨慕的；嫉妒的
get to V. 得以～；能夠～
have fun 玩得愉快　　practice〔'præktɪs〕*n.* 練習
safari〔 sə'fɑrɪ 〕*n.* 狩獵旅行

TEST 8

第一部分：辨識句意（第 1-10 題，共 10 題）

作答說明：第 1-10 題每題均有三個選項，請依據所聽到的單句，選出
符合描述的圖片。

示例題：你會看到

(A) 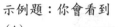 (B) (C)

依據所播放的內容，正確答案應該選 A，請將答案紙該題「Ⓐ」
的地方塗黑、塗滿，即 ●ⒷⒸ。

1. (A)  (B)  (C)

2. (A)  (B)  (C)

3. (A)   (B)   (C)

4. (A)   (B)   (C)

5. (A)   (B)   (C)

6. (A)   (B)   (C)

7. (A)   (B)   (C)

8. (A)　　　　　(B)　　　　　(C)

9. (A)　　　　　(B)　　　　　(C)

10. (A)　　　　　(B)　　　　　(C)

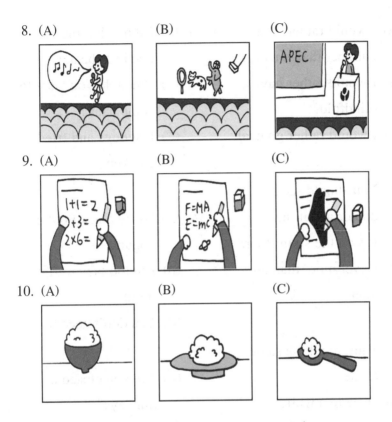

第二部分：基本問答（第 11-20 題，共 10 題）

作答說明：第 11-20 題每題均有三個選項，請依據所聽到的對話問句，選出一個最適合的回答。

示例題：你會看到

(A) She is talking to the teacher.

(B) She is a student in my class.

(C) She is wearing a beautiful dress.

依據所播放的內容，正確答案應該選 B，請將答案紙該題「Ⓑ」的地方塗黑、塗滿，即Ⓐ●Ⓒ。

11. (A) I would rather be a hammer than a nail.
    (B) I would rather have a blindfold.
    (C) I would rather go deaf.

12. (A) You should see a doctor about that.
    (B) It's on the sixth floor.
    (C) Never more than an hour.

13. (A) They're all the same to me.
    (B) Once in a while.
    (C) No problem.

14. (A) It's coming from the kitchen.
    (B) I don't know.
    (C) I'll show you to your table.

15. (A) I'd much rather see one in a theater.
    (B) When do you want to come back?
    (C) Hot dogs and fried chicken.

16. (A) We're almost out of yogurt.
    (B) I'm too lazy to figure it out.
    (C) You don't need it.

17. (A) Are you closed on Sundays?
    (B) Is there something you can do?
    (C) Will I have to show any ID?

18. (A) Twice a day.

 (B) Round-trip.

 (C) Back and forth.

19. (A) Thanks for the warning.

 (B) You are very welcome.

 (C) He is in the elevator.

20. (A) I forgot my book.

 (B) You can't tell him anything.

 (C) Cool! I'll read it this weekend.

第三部分：言談理解（第 21-30 題，共 10 題）

作答說明： 第 21-30 題每題均有三個選項，請依據所聽到的對話或短文內容，選出一個最適合的答案。

示例題：你會看到

(A) 9:50.　　(B) 10:00.　　(C) 10:10.

依據所播放的內容，正確答案應該選 B，請將答案紙該題「Ⓑ」的地方塗黑、塗滿，即Ⓐ●Ⓒ。

---

21. (A) In a department store.

 (B) In a restaurant.

 (C) In a bus station.

22. (A) Travel.

 (B) Economics.

 (C) Food.

23. (A) He studied as hard as he could.
    (B) He received a passing score.
    (C) He failed miserably.

24. (A) Yes.
    (B) No.
    (C) It's impossible to say.

25. (A) Complain about an employee.
    (B) Return the items for store credit.
    (C) Learn more about the store's policies.

26. (A) To start a family.
    (B) Her family was against it.
    (C) Three months ago.

27. (A) 10 years old.
    (B) 12 years old.
    (C) 22 years old.

28. (A) She has body issues.
    (B) She has trouble paying attention.
    (C) She has multiple personalities.

29. (A) Read aloud what is written on the board.
    (B) Go back to playing Angry Birds on his iPhone.
    (C) Help the woman find her glasses.

30. (A) On a college campus.
    (B) On a crowded bus.
    (C) In a city bus terminal.

TEST 8 詳解

第一部分:辨識句意

1. (**C**) (A)  (B)  (C)

Fred listens to music on his personal computer.
弗雷德在他的個人電腦上聽音樂。

* ***listen to*** 聽　　music〔'mjuzɪk〕*n.* 音樂
personal〔'pɝsn̩ḷ〕*adj.* 個人的
computer〔kəm'pjutɚ〕*n.* 電腦

2. (**B**) (A)  (B)  (C)

The movie is a love story. 電影是個愛情故事。

* movie〔'muvɪ〕*n.* 電影　　love〔lʌv〕*n.* 愛;愛情
story〔'storɪ〕*n.* 故事

3. (**B**) (A)  (B)  (C)

The boys are playing cards. 男孩在玩紙牌。

* cards〔kɑrdz〕n. 紙牌遊戲

4.(**A**) (A)   (B)   (C)

Priscilla is brushing her teeth. 普莉希拉正在刷牙。

* brush〔brʌʃ〕v. 刷   teeth〔tiθ〕n. 牙齒【單數為 tooth】

5.(**C**) (A)   (B)   (C)

My sister spends a lot of time in the bathroom.
我妹妹花很多時間在浴室裡。

* spend〔spɛnd〕v. 花（時間、金錢等）
  a lot of 很多   bathroom〔'bæθ,rum〕n. 浴室；廁所

6.(**B**) (A)   (B)   (C)

Louise is wearing pants and a shirt. 露易絲穿著長褲和襯衫。

* pants〔pænts〕n. pl. 褲子；長褲   shirt〔ʃɜt〕n. 襯衫

7. (**C**) (A)  (B)  (C)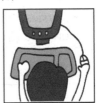

I spend most of my free time surfing the Internet.
我大多的空閒時間都在上網。

* spend〔spɛnd〕*v.* 花（時間、金錢等）
  free time 空閒時間　　surf〔sɝf〕*v.* 瀏覽
  Internet〔'ɪntɚ,nɛt〕*n.* 網際網路

8. (**C**) (A)  (B)  (C)

We attended a lecture about economics.
我們參加一個關於經濟學的演講。

* attend〔ə'tɛnd〕*v.* 出席；參加
  lecture〔'lɛktʃɚ〕*n.* 演講
  economics〔,ikə'nɑmɪks〕*n.* 經濟學

9. (**B**) (A)  (B)  (C)

Physics is my favorite subject. 物理是我最喜愛的科目。

* physics (ˈfɪzɪks) *n.* 物理學
favorite (ˈfevərɪt) *adj.* 最喜愛的　　subject (ˈsʌbdʒɪkt) *n.* 科目

10. (**C**) (A)　　　　　　(B)　　　　　　(C)

Here's a spoonful of rice. 這裡有一匙飯。

* spoonful (ˈspunˌful) *n.* 一匙的量　　rice (raɪs) *n.* 米;米飯

第二部分：基本問答

11. (**C**) I never thought about it that way. Would you rather go deaf or blind? 我從沒那樣想過。你寧可聾了還是瞎了？

(A) I would rather be a hammer than a nail.
我寧可當鐵鎚也不願當釘子。

(B) I would rather have a blindfold. 我寧可戴上眼罩。

(C) I would rather go deaf. 我寧可聾了。

* ***think about*** 考慮;思考　　***that way*** 那樣 (= *in that way*)
would rather 寧願　　go (go) *v.* 變得
deaf (dɛf) *adj.* 聾的;聽不見的　　blind (blaɪnd) *adj.* 瞎的
blindfold (ˈblaɪndˌfold) *n.* 眼罩
hammer (ˈhæmɚ) *n.* 鐵鎚　　nail (nel) *n.* 釘子
would rather be a hammer than a nail 寧可當鎚子也不要當
釘子 (= *would rather be active than passive*)【原為歌詞，
鎚子象徵「主動」，釘子象徵「被動」】

12. (**B**) I'm looking for Dr. Nelson's office. Can you tell me where it is?
我正在找尼爾森醫生的診所。你可以告訴我在哪裡嗎？

(A) You should see a doctor about that.
關於那件事，你應該去看醫生。

(B) It's on the sixth floor. 在六樓。

(C) Never more than an hour. 從沒有超過一小時。

* **look for** 尋找　　office〔'ɔfɪs〕n. 辦公室；診所
  see a doctor 看醫生　　floor〔flor〕n. 層樓

13. (**C**) Ah! The battery is dead. May I borrow your cell phone?
啊！電池沒電了。可以跟你借手機嗎？

(A) They're all the same to me. 他們對我來說都一樣。

(B) Once in a while. 偶爾。

(C) No problem. 沒問題。

* ah〔ɑ〕interj. （表示悲、喜、痛苦等）啊
  battery〔'bætərɪ〕n. 電池　　dead〔dɛd〕adj. 沒電的
  borrow〔'baro〕v. 借（入）　　**cell phone** 手機
  once in a while 偶爾；有時候（= *sometimes*）
  No problem. 沒問題。

14. (**C**) Yes, I have a reservation at 8:15 for three people. The name is Swanson.
是的，我有預訂八點十五分，三個人。名字是史旺森。

(A) It's coming from the kitchen. 這是來自廚房。

(B) I don't know. 我不知道。

(C) I'll show you to your table. 我會帶你到你的桌子。

* reservation〔ˌrɛzə'veʃən〕n. 預約
  kitchen〔'kɪtʃɪn〕n. 廚房　　show〔ʃo〕v. 引導…到

15. (**A**) There's nothing on television tonight. Let's download a movie. 今晚電視沒什麼可看的。我們來下載電影吧。

(A) I'd much rather see one in a theater.
我寧可去電影院看。

(B) When do you want to come back?
你什麼時會要回來？

(C) Hot dogs and fried chicken. 熱狗和炸雞。

* television〔ˈtɛləˌvɪʒən〕*n.* 電視
let's + *V.* 我們一起~吧　　download〔ˈdaʊnˌlod〕*v.* 下載
would much rather~ 更希望~
theater〔ˈθiətɚ〕*n.* 電影院　　*hot dog* 熱狗
fried〔fraɪd〕*adj.* 油炸的　　chicken〔ˈtʃɪkɪn〕*n.* 雞肉

16. (**A**) I'm going to the market. Can you think of anything we need? 我正要去市場。你有想到我們需要什麼嗎？

(A) We're almost out of yogurt.
我們的優格快要沒了。

(B) I'm too lazy to figure it out. 我太懶，想不出來。

(C) You don't need it. 你不需要這東西。

* market〔ˈmɑrkɪt〕*n.* 市場　　*think of* 想到
almost〔ˈɔlˌmost〕*adv.* 幾乎　　*be out of* 沒有…
yogurt〔ˈjogɚt〕*n.* 優格
too~to… 太~無法…　　lazy〔ˈlezɪ〕*adj.* 懶惰的
figure out 想出；理解　　need〔nid〕*v.* 需要

17. (**C**) Once you've filled out the application, take it to window 13. 你一填寫好申請書，就拿到十三號窗口。

(A) Are you closed on Sundays? 你們週日沒開嗎？

(B) Is there something you can do? 有什麼事是你能做的？

(C) Will I have to show any ID?
我必須出示任何身份證明嗎？

* once〔wʌns〕*conj.* 一旦；一…就　　*fill out* 填寫
application〔ˌæpləˈkeʃən〕*n.* 申請書
ID 身份證明 (= *identification*)

18. (**A**) Do you know how often the ferry goes to Hong Kong?

你知道輪船多久去一次香港嗎？

(A) Twice a day. 一天兩次。

(B) Round-trip. 來回的。

(C) Back and forth. 來來回回地。

* ***how often*** 多久一次　　ferry〔'fɛrɪ〕*n.* 渡輪
Hong Kong〔'hɑŋ'kɑŋ〕香港
round-trip〔'raʊnd,trɪp〕*adj.* 來回的
back and forth 來來回回地（*= to and fro*）

19. (**A**) Oh, Jason, before you go… The elevator is out of order. You'll have to take the stairs.

喔，傑森，在你還沒走之前…電梯故障了。你得爬樓梯。

(A) Thanks for the warning. 謝謝你的提醒。

(B) You are very welcome. 不客氣。

(C) He is in the elevator. 他在電梯裡。

* elevator〔'ɛlə,vetɚ〕*n.* 電梯　　***out of order*** 故障
take the stairs 爬樓梯　　***thanks for*** 謝謝你…
warning〔'wɔrnɪŋ〕*n.* 提醒；警告
elevator〔'ɛlə,vetɚ〕*n.* 電梯

20. (**C**) Here's that book I've been telling you about.

這是我一直跟你說的那本書。

(A) I forgot my book. 我忘記帶書。

(B) You can't tell him anything. 你不能跟他說任何事情。

(C) Cool! I'll read it this weekend.

好酷喔，我這個週末可以讀。

* forgot〔fɚ'gɑt〕*v.* 忘記【forget 的過去式】
cool〔kul〕*adj.* 很酷的；很棒的
weekend〔'wik'ɛnd〕*n.* 週末

第三部分：言談理解

21. (**B**)　W : God, I can't stand this place. It's filthy and the
　　　　　　　waiters are rude.

　　女：天啊，我無法忍受這個地方。這裡很髒，而且服務生很沒
　　　　禮貌。

　　M : Come on, Mary. They serve the best deep-dish pizza
　　　　in Northern California.

　　男：算了吧，瑪麗。在加州北部他們提供最好的厚底比薩。

　　W : That's no excuse for poor sanitation and bad service.

　　女：那不是衛生不佳和服務不好的藉口。

　　Question : Where did this conversation most likely take
　　　　　　　place? 這個對話最可能發生在哪裡？

　　(A) In a department store. 在百貨公司裡。

　　(B) In a restaurant. 在餐廳裡

　　(C) In a bus station. 在公車站。

* God〔gɑd〕*interj.*【表示驚訝、痛苦等】天啊！
　stand〔stænd〕*v.* 忍受　　filthy〔'fɪlθɪ〕*adj.* 骯髒的
　waiter〔'wetɚ〕*n.* 服務生　　rude〔rud〕*adj.* 無禮的
　Come on.【表示催促、懇求】好吧；算了吧。
　serve〔sɜv〕*v.* 供應
　northern〔'nɔrðən〕*adj.* 北方的；北部的
　deep-dish pizza 厚底披薩
　California〔ˌkælə'fɔrnjə〕*n.* 加州【位於美國西海岸】
　excuse〔ɪk'skjus〕*n.* 藉口
　poor〔pur〕*adj.* 差勁的　　service〔'sɜvɪs〕*n.* 服務
　conversation〔ˌkɑnvə'seʃən〕*n.* 對話
　likely〔'laɪklɪ〕*adv.* 可能地　　***take place*** 發生；出現
　restaurant〔'rɛstərənt〕*n.* 餐廳
　bus station 公車站

22. (**A**)　M : Summer is tourist season in Rome. All the hotels are booked, the restaurants are full, and the prices go through the roof.

男：夏季是羅馬的旅遊旺季。所有的飯店都被預訂一空，餐廳滿座，而且價格一飛沖天。

W : Maybe I should schedule a visit in early fall?

女：或許我應該計畫早秋的行程嗎？

M : That's probably a better idea than say, July.

男：那可能會是比較好的主意，比起像是七月這時候。

Question : What are the speakers mainly discussing?

　　　　　說話者主要在討論什麼？

(A) Travel. 旅行。

(B) Economics. 經濟學。

(C) Food. 食物。

* tourist〔'turɪst〕 *adj.* 觀光的；旅遊的
  season〔'sizn̩〕 *n.* 季節；時期
  Rome〔rom〕 *n.* 羅馬【義大利首都】
  hotel〔ho'tɛl〕 *n.* 飯店；旅館
  book〔buk〕 *v.* 預訂
  price〔praɪs〕 *n.* 價格
  roof〔ruf〕 *n.* 屋頂
  go through the roof 迅速增加；高漲【也有「大發雷霆」的意思】
  schedule〔'skɛdʒul〕 *v.* 排定
  visit〔'vɪzɪt〕 *n.* 參觀；旅行　　fall〔fɔl〕 *n.* 秋天
  probably〔'prɑbəblɪ〕 *adv.* 可能
  say〔se〕 *v.* 比如說；例如（= *let's say*）【用作插入語】
  mainly〔'menlɪ〕 *adv.* 主要地
  discuss〔dɪ'skʌs〕 *v.* 討論
  travel〔'trævl̩〕 *n.* 旅行
  economics〔ˌikə'nɑmɪks〕 *n.* 經濟學

23. (**B**) W : How did you do on the physics mid-term? You studied quite a bit, didn't you?

女：你物理期中考考得如何？你很用功，不是嗎？

M : Yeah, I did. But I don't think it made much of a difference. I barely passed with a 63.

男：是呀，我有。不過我不覺得有什麼很大的差別。我勉強通過考試，63 分。

W : Wow, that's worse than I did. Maybe you should re-think your study methods.

女：哇，比我考得還要差。或許你應該重新思考你的讀書方法。

Question : How did the man do on the exam?

男士考試考得如何？

(A) He studied as hard as he could. 他盡他所能用功讀書。

(B) He received a passing score. 他得到及格分數。

(C) He failed miserably. 他考得很差沒及格。

* physics〔ˈfɪzɪks〕*n.* 物理學

mid-term〔ˈmɪd͵tɝm〕*n.* 期中考

quite a bit 很多；相當大（*= a lot*）

not much of a… 不怎麼好的…；稱不上…

difference〔ˈdɪfərəns〕*n.* 差別；不同

make a difference 有差別；有影響

barely〔ˈbɛrlɪ〕*adv.* 勉強地；僅僅

pass〔pæs〕*v.*（考試）及格

maybe〔ˈmebi〕*adv.* 或許；可能

method〔ˈmɛθəd〕*n.* 方法

as…***as one can*** 儘可能…

receive〔rɪˈsiv〕*v.* 收到；得到

score〔skor〕*n.* 分數

fail〔fel〕*v.*（考試）不及格

miserably〔ˈmɪzərəblɪ〕*adv.* 悲慘地

24. (**B**) M : These cookies are delicious! Did you make these,
Helen?

男：這些餅乾很好吃！妳做的嗎，海倫？

W : No, I bought them at a bakery. You like them, huh?

女：不，我在麵包店買的。你喜歡嗎？

M : They are the best cookies I've ever tasted!

男：它們是我吃過最好吃的餅乾！

Question : Did Helen make the cookies?

　　海倫做了餅乾嗎？

(A) Yes. 是的。

(B) No. 不是。

(C) It's impossible to say. 很難說。

* cookie〔ˈkʊkɪ〕n. 餅乾　　delicious〔dɪˈlɪʃəs〕adj. 美味的
bought〔bɔt〕v. 買【三態為：buy-bought-bought】
bakery〔ˈbekərɪ〕n. 麵包店
huh〔hʌ〕interj.【表示驚奇、不贊同、疑問等】哈！
taste〔test〕v. 品嚐；吃
impossible〔ɪmˈpɑsəb!〕adj. 不可能的；難以…的

25. (**B**) W : I'd like to return these items. Here's my receipt.

女：我想要退還這些物品。這是我的收據。

M : Sorry, ma'am. All sales are final. I can give you
store credit, but no cash back on returned items.

男：很抱歉，小姐。貨物既出，概不退還。我可以給妳店內信用
點數，但退換物品無法換成現金。

W : I understand the policy. I'll take the store credit.

女：我了解這政策。我接受店內信用點數。

Question : What does the woman want to do?

　　女士想要做什麼？

(A) Complain about an employee.

抱怨一位員工。

(B) Return the items for store credit.

退還物品換店內信用點數。

(C) Learn more about the store's policies.

知道更多店裡的政策。

* *would like to V.* 想要~
return〔rɪ'tɝn〕 v. 退回
item〔'aɪtəm〕 n. 物品；項目
receipt〔rɪ'sit〕 n. 收據
ma'am〔mæm〕 n. 小姐；太太（= *madam*）
sales〔selz〕 n. 出售；拍賣
final〔'faɪn̩〕 adj. 最終的
All sales are final. 貨物既出，概不退還。
understand〔ˌʌndɚ'stænd〕 v. 了解
policy〔'pɑləsɪ〕 n. 政策　　take〔tek〕 v. 接受
credit〔'krɛdɪt〕 n. 信用；帳戶餘額
store credit 店內信用點數
complain〔kəm'plen〕 v. 抱怨
employee〔ˌɛmplɔɪ'i〕 n. 員工　　learn〔lɝn〕 v. 知道

26. (**C**) M : Did you hear the news? John and Mary are having a baby.

男：妳有聽到新聞嗎？約翰和瑪麗要生小孩了。

W : They are? Wow, that was fast. They've only been married what, three months?

女：是嗎？哇，那麼快。他們才結婚，嗯，三個月吧？

M : Well, John has always said he wanted to start a family. Now's his chance.

男：嗯，約翰總是說他想要組織一個家庭。現在他的機會來了。

Question : When did John and Mary get married?

約翰和瑪麗何時結婚的？

(A) To start a family. 爲了組織一個家庭。

(B) Her family was against it. 她的家人反對。

(C) Three months ago. 三個月前。

* ***have a baby*** 生小孩

married〔'mærɪd〕*adj.* 結婚的

what〔hwɑt〕*interj.* 哦【用於想數字或數量而暫停】

start a family 組織一個家庭；生第一個小孩

chance〔tʃæns〕*n.* 機會   against〔ə'gɛnst〕*prep.* 反對

27. (**C**) W : How long have you been playing the piano?

女：你彈鋼琴多久了？

M : Well, I started when I was 12, so about 10 years, I think.

男：嗯，我十二歲開始彈的，所以大概十年了，我想。

W : You're really quite good. Would you play me another song?

女：你彈得真的很好。你要再彈另一首歌給我聽嗎？

Question : How old is the man now?

男士現在幾歲？

(A) 10 years old. 十歲。

(B) 12 years old. 十二歲。

(C) 22 years old. 二十二歲。

* quite〔kwaɪt〕*adv.* 相當；非常

28. (**B**) M : What did the psychologist say?

男：心理學家說什麼？

W : Well, he thinks Suzie has attention issues. She has trouble focusing on one thing for any length of time.

女：嗯，他說蘇西有注意力方面的問題。她很難專注某件事持續一段時間。

M : And? What can be done about that?

男：還有呢？可以做些什麼來解決嗎？

Question : What is Suzie's problem?

蘇西有什麼問題？

(A) She has body issues. 她有身體上的問題。

(B) She has trouble paying attention.

她很難專心。

(C) She has multiple personalities.

她有多重人格。

* psychologist〔saɪˋkɑlədʒɪst〕*n.* 心理學家

attention〔əˋtɛnʃən〕*n.* 專心；注意力

issue〔ˋɪʃʊ〕*n.* 問題　　***have troube + V-ing*** 很難~

focus〔ˋfokəs〕*v.* 集中；專心＜*on*＞

length〔lɛŋθ〕*n.* 長度；期間　　body〔ˋbɑdɪ〕*n.* 身體

pay〔pe〕*v.* 付出　　***pay attention*** 專心

multiple〔ˋmʌltəpḷ〕*adj.* 多重的

personality〔͵pɝsṇˋælətɪ〕*n.* 個性

multiple personalities 多重人格【同一人身上出現兩種或多種不同的人格，而且兩種人格各有自己的特色】

29.(**A**) W : May I see a menu, please?

女：我可以看一下菜單嗎？

M : We don't have a paper menu. Everything we have is listed up on the board.

男：我們沒有紙本菜單。我們有的東西都列在看板上。

W : I don't have my glasses with me so I can't read it.
　　　Would you...be able to...tell me...?

女：我沒有戴眼鏡，所以我看不到。你…可以…告訴我…嗎？

Question : What will the man most likely do next?

　　　　　男士接下來最可能做什麼？

(A) Read aloud what is written on the board.

　　大聲唸出寫在看板上的東西。

(B) Go back to playing Angry Birds on his iPhone.

　　回去玩他 iPhone 上的憤怒鳥。

(C) Help the woman find her glasses.

　　幫助女士找她的眼鏡。

* menu〔'mɛnju〕*n.* 菜單
　paper〔'pepɚ〕*adj.* 紙的；紙製的
　list〔lɪst〕*v.* 列出
　board〔bord〕*n.* 木板；佈告板
　glasses〔'glæzɪs〕*n. pl.* 眼鏡
　able〔'ebḷ〕*adj.* 能夠…的
　be able to V. 能夠…
　read〔rid〕*v.* 讀給…聽；唸出
　aloud〔ə'laud〕*adv.* 出聲地
　go back to V-ing 恢復～；重新～
　Angry Birds 憤怒鳥【益智遊戲】
　help *sb.* ***(to) V.*** 幫助某人（做）

30. (**A**) M : So, Laura, what's it like being the new girl on
　　　　　campus? Are you having any trouble finding your
　　　　　way around?

男：這麼說，蘿拉，在校園裡當個新來的女生感覺如何？在找
　　路方面妳有任何困難嗎？

W：It's been great so far, Jack. Everyone has been so
　　friendly and helpful.

女：目前都還很好，傑克。每個人都很友善，也願意幫忙。

M：Let me give you my cell phone number and maybe
　　we could hang out sometime.

男：讓我給妳我的手機號碼，或許哪一天我們可以一起出來逛
　　一逛。

Question：Where is this conversation most likely taking
　　　　　　place? 這對話最可能出現在哪裡？

(A) On a college campus. 在大學校園裡。

(B) On a crowded bus. 在擁擠的公車上。

(C) In a city bus terminal. 在市區的公車總站。

* so〔so〕adv. 如此看來
  What's ~like? ～如何？
  campus〔ˈkæmpəs〕n. 校園
  on campus 在校園裡
  have trouble + V-ing 很難～
  find one's **way around** 知道去哪的路；對…很熟悉（= know
    one's way around）
  so far 到目前為止
  friendly〔ˈfrɛndlɪ〕adj. 友善的
  helpful〔ˈhɛlpfəl〕adj. 主動幫忙的
  cell phone 手機電
  hang out 閒逛；閒蕩
  sometime〔ˈsʌmˌtaɪm〕adv. 某一天；某時
  college〔ˈkɑlɪdʒ〕n. 大學
  crowded〔ˈkraʊdɪd〕adj. 擁擠的
  terminal〔ˈtɝmənḷ〕n. 終點站；總站

TEST 9

第一部分：辨識句意（第 1-10 題，共 10 題）

作答說明：第 1-10 題每題均有三個選項，請依據所聽到的單句，選出符合描述的圖片。

示例題：你會看到

(A)   (B)   (C)

依據所播放的內容，正確答案應該選 A，請將答案紙該題「Ⓐ」的地方塗黑、塗滿，即 ●ⒷⒸ。

1. (A)   (B)   (C)

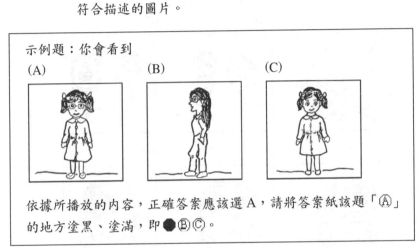

2. (A)   (B)   (C)

3. (A)   (B)   (C)

4. (A)   (B)   (C)

5. (A)   (B)   (C)

6. (A)   (B)   (C)

7. (A)   (B)   (C)

8. (A)　　　　　　(B)　　　　　　(C)

9. (A)　　　　　　(B)　　　　　　(C)

10. (A)　　　　　　(B)　　　　　　(C)

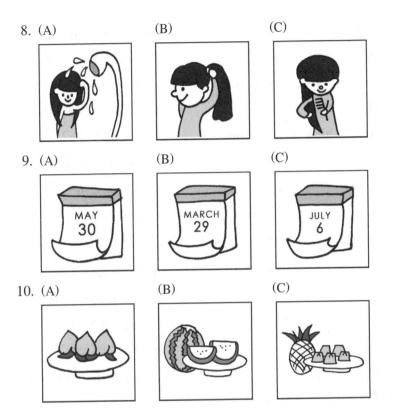

第二部分：基本問答（第 11-20 題，共 10 題）

作答說明： 第 11-20 題每題均有三個選項，請依據所聽到的對話問句，選出一個最適合的回答。

示例題：你會看到

(A) She is talking to the teacher.

(B) She is a student in my class.

(C) She is wearing a beautiful dress.

依據所播放的內容，正確答案應該選 B，請將答案紙該題「Ⓑ」的地方塗黑、塗滿，即 Ⓐ●Ⓒ。

11. (A) It used to be the tallest building in the world.
    (B) I don't. You should ask the driver.
    (C) Yes, I think it looks fine.

12. (A) Jobs are hard to find these days.
    (B) Check your computer.
    (C) Let me take a look at it.

13. (A) I didn't think it was on.
    (B) Call 9-1-1.
    (C) No, thanks. I've got homework to do.

14. (A) I'm afraid it does not.
    (B) I'm feeling a little blue myself.
    (C) I'm hoping they won't notice.

15. (A) She likes music, doesn't she? Buy her a CD.
    (B) She plays tennis, doesn't she? Take her to a ball.
    (C) She doesn't read poetry.

16. (A) I can lend you some money until we get back.
    (B) You can stay in my room after the party.
    (C) Admission to the museum is free.

17. (A) She has long brown hair and green eyes.
    (B) The stores are all closed.
    (C) Let's ask him if he needs any help.

18. (A) I hope you saved some money for the taxi.
    (B) I hope you saved some time to read my essay.
    (C) I hope you saved some room for dessert.

19. (A) How? I thought it was a done deal.
    (B) Where? I thought they were finished.
    (C) Why? I thought you two got along.

20. (A) Pay up.
    (B) Don't mention it.
    (C) Likewise, I'm sure.

第三部分：言談理解（第 21-30 題，共 10 題）

作答說明：第 21-30 題每題均有三個選項，請依據所聽到的對話或短文內容，選出一個最適合的答案。

示例題：你會看到

(A) 9:50.   (B) 10:00.   (C) 10:10.

依據所播放的內容，正確答案應該選 B，請將答案紙該題「Ⓑ」的地方塗黑、塗滿，即 Ⓐ●Ⓒ。

---

21. (A) To learn more about depressing events.
    (B) To keep up with current events.
    (C) To help prepare for future events.

22. (A) Classmates.
    (B) Colleagues.
    (C) Siblings.

23. (A) St. Louis.
    (B) On a plane.
    (C) In an airport.

24. (A) Insulted.
    (B) Regretful.
    (C) Silly.

25. (A) He's not a very good actor.
    (B) He's too young to retire.
    (C) He's very handsome.

26. (A) Mail a package.
    (B) Check out a book.
    (C) Fill up his gas tank.

27. (A) His time is limited.
    (B) His children are special.
    (C) His pants are too tight.

28. (A) Watch the sunset.
    (B) Motivate the man to get more exercise.
    (C) Wake up early tomorrow morning.

29. (A) She will call the manager.
    (B) She will apologize for stealing the man's wallet.
    (C) She will see the man to his table.

30. (A) It is very playful.
    (B) It is hungry.
    (C) It is on public property.

TEST 9 詳解

第一部分：辨識句意

1. (**C**) (A)  (B)  (C)

Would you like a slice of my homemade pie?
你想要一片我自製的派嗎？

* **would like** 想要　　slice〔slaɪs〕 *n.* 片
homemade〔'hom'med〕 *adj.* 自製的；自家做的
pie〔paɪ〕 *n.* 派

2. (**C**) (A)  (B)  (C)

Peter plays the violin.　彼得拉小提琴。
* violin〔ˌvaɪə'lɪn〕 *n.* 小提琴

3. (**A**) (A)  (B)  (C)

Let's watch television. 我們來看電視吧。

* ***let's + V.*** 我們一起~吧
  television〔ˈtɛləˌvɪʒən〕*n.* 電視

4. (**A**) (A)　　　　　　 (B)　　　　　　 (C)

John prefers to travel by train. 約翰偏好坐火車旅行。

* prefer〔prɪˈfɝ〕*v.* 比較喜歡;偏好　　travel〔ˈtrævl̩〕*v.* 旅行
  train〔tren〕*n.* 火車　***by train*** 坐火車

5. (**A**) (A)　　　　　　 (B)　　　　　　 (C)

Nina has new pair of eyeglasses. 妮娜戴了一副新眼鏡。

* pair〔pɛr〕*n.* 一副;一雙　　eyeglasses〔ˈaɪˌglæzɪs〕*n. pl.* 眼鏡

6. (**A**) (A)　　　　　　 (B)　　　　　　 (C)

Mary is wearing a scarf. 瑪麗戴著一條圍巾。

* wear〔wɛr〕*v.* 戴著　　scarf〔skɑrf〕*n.* 圍巾

7. (**B**) (A)  (B) 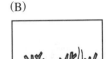 (C)

The trees are bare during the winter months.

在冬天那幾個月的時候，樹光禿禿的。

* bare〔bɛr〕*adj.* 沒樹葉的；光禿禿的
  during〔'dʊrɪŋ〕*prep.* 在…期間
  winter〔'wɪntɚ〕*n.* 冬天　　month〔mʌnθ〕*n.* 月

8. (**C**) (A)  (B)  (C)

Debbie is brushing her hair.　黛比在梳頭髮。

* brush〔brʌʃ〕*v.* 刷；梳　　hair〔hɛr〕*n.* 頭髮

9. (**A**) (A)  (B)  (C)

Call me on May 30th.　5 月 30 日打電話給我。

* call〔kɔl〕*v.* 打電話給（某人）
  May〔me〕*n.* 五月

10. (**C**) (A)  (B) (C)

Don't you just love pineapple? 你不是很愛鳳梨嗎？

* pineapple〔'paɪnˌæpl̩〕*n.* 鳳梨

第二部分：基本問答

11. (**B**) Excuse me. Do you know if this bus stops at Taipei 101?
對不起。你知道這台公車是否有停台北 101 嗎？

(A) It used to be the tallest building in the world.
它以前是世界最高的建築物。

(B) I don't. You should ask the driver.
我不知道。你應該問司機。

(C) Yes, I think it looks fine.
是的，我覺得它看起來很好。

* *Excuse me*. 對不起。【用於引起對方的注意】
used to V. 以前~　　building〔'bɪldɪŋ〕*n.* 建築物
driver〔'draɪvɚ〕*n.* 駕駛人；司機　　look〔lʊk〕*v.* 看起來

12. (**C**) There's something wrong with my computer. It's not
working. 我的電腦有問題。它不動了。

(A) Jobs are hard to find these days.
最近工作很難找。

(B) Check your computer.
檢查你的電腦。

(C) Let me take a look at it. 讓我看一下。

* ***There is something wrong with~*** ～出了問題；～狀況不好
work〔wɜk〕v. 運作；運轉　　job〔dʒɑb〕n. 工作
these days 現在；目前　　check〔tʃɛk〕v. 檢查
compute〔kəm'pjutɚ〕n. 電腦
take a look at 看一下…

13. (**C**) We're going to watch the fireworks. Would you care to
join us? 我們要去看煙火。你想要加入我們嗎？

　　(A) I didn't think it was on. 我不覺得這是開著的。

　　(B) Call 9-1-1 打 911。

　　(C) No, thanks. I've got homework to do.
　　　　不，謝謝。我有功課要做。

　　* fireworks〔'faɪr,wɜks〕n. pl. 煙火　　***care to V.*** 想要~
　　join〔dʒɔɪn〕v. 加入　　on〔ɑn〕adj. 開著的

14. (**A**) I really like this shirt except for the color. Does it come
in blue?
我真的很喜歡這件襯衫，除了它的顏色。它有藍色的嗎？

　　(A) I'm afraid it does not. 恐怕沒有。

　　(B) I'm feeling a little blue myself.
　　　　我今天感到有點憂鬱。

　　(C) I'm hoping they won't notice.
　　　　我希望他們不會注意到。

　　* shirt〔ʃɜt〕n. 襯衫　　***except for*** 除了…以外
　　come in 有~　　***I'm afraid*** ~【表示遺憾】恐怕~
　　blue〔blu〕adj. 憂鬱的　　hope〔hop〕v. 希望
　　notice〔'notɪs〕v. 注意到

15. (**A**) Rachel's birthday is next week and I have no idea what
to get her.
瑞秋的生日在下週，而我不知道要買什麼給她。

(A) She likes music, doesn't she? Buy her a CD.

她喜歡音樂，不是嗎？買張 CD 給她。

(B) She plays tennis, doesn't she? Take her to a ball.

她打網球，不是嗎？帶她去舞會。

(C) She doens't read poetry.

她不讀詩。

* **have no idea** 不知道　　get〔gɛt〕v. 買給（某人）（某物）
music〔'mjuzɪk〕n. 音樂
tennis〔'tɛnɪs〕n. 網球　　ball〔bɔl〕n. 舞會
poetry〔'po·ɪtrɪ〕n. 【總稱】詩

16. (**A**) Oh, no! I think I left my wallet back at the hotel.

喔，不！我想我把皮夾留在旅館了。

(A) I can lend you some money until we get back.

直到我們回來之前，我可以借你一些錢。

(B) You can stay in my room after the party.

派對結束後，你可以待在我房裡。

(C) Admission to the museum is free. 博物館免費入場。

* left〔lɛft〕v. 遺留【leave 的過去式】
wallet〔'wɑlɪt〕n. 皮夾
back〔bæk〕adv. 在原處　　hotel〔ho'tɛl〕n. 飯店；旅館
lend〔lɛnd〕v. 借（出）
admission〔əd'mɪʃən〕n. 入場許可 < to >
museum〔mju'ziəm〕n. 博物館　　free〔fri〕adj. 免費的

17. (**C**) That little boy looks lost. I wonder where his mother is.

那小男孩看似迷路了。不知道他媽媽在哪裡。

(A) She has long brown hair and green eyes.

她有棕色長髮，綠色眼睛。

(B) The stores are all closed. 商店都關了。

(C) Let's ask him if he needs any help.

我們來問他是否需要幫忙。

* look〔lʊk〕v. 看起來　　lost〔lɔst〕adj. 迷路的
wonder〔'wʌndɚ〕v. 想知道
brown〔braʊn〕adj. 棕色的　　store〔stor〕n. 商店
***let's* + V.** 我們一起～吧

18. (**C**) The meal was delightful. I'm stuffed! 餐點很棒。我很飽！

(A) I hope you saved some money for the taxi.

我希望你留些錢坐計程車。

(B) I hope you saved some time to read my essay.

我希望你保留一些時間看我的文章。

(C) I hope you saved some room for dessert.

我希望你留點空間吃甜點。

* meal〔mil〕n. 餐點
delightful〔dɪ'laɪtfəl〕adj. 令人愉快的
stuffed〔stʌft〕adj. 飽的　　save〔sev〕v. 保留；節省
taxi〔'tæksɪ〕n. 計程車　　essay〔'ɛse〕n. 論說文；文章
room〔rum〕n. 空間　　dessert〔dɪ'zɜt〕n. 甜點

19. (**C**) My brother is coming for a visit next week. I'm not looking forward to it.

我弟弟下週要來拜訪我。我並不期待他來。

(A) How? I thought it was a done deal.

怎麼會？我以為這已成定局。

(B) Where? I thought they were finished.

在哪裡？我以為他們做完了。

(C) Why? I thought you two got along.

為什麼？我以為你們倆處得很好。

* visit〔'vɪzɪt〕 *n.* 拜訪　 ***look forward to*** 期待
done〔dʌn〕 *adj.* 完成的；結束的　　deal〔dil〕 *n.* 協議；交易
a done deal 已成定局的事；無法改變的事
It's a done deal. 生米煮成熟飯；木已成舟。
finished〔'fɪnɪʃt〕 *adj.* 做完的；完蛋的
get along 和睦相處

20. (**B**) Thanks for the ride, Nick. I owe you one.

謝謝你載我一程，尼克。我欠你一次。

(A) Pay up. 付清。

(B) Don't mention it. 不客氣。

(C) Likewise, I'm sure 同樣地，我確定。

* ride〔raɪd〕 *n.* 搭乘；搭便車
owe〔o〕 *v.* 欠　 ***I owe you one.*** 我欠你一次人情。
pay up 付清；全部還清　　mention〔'mɛnʃən〕 *v.* 提到
Don't mention it. 不客氣。
likewise〔'laɪk,waɪz〕 *adv.* 同樣地

第三部分：言談理解

21. (**B**) W : The news is so depressing. Every time I turn it on,
there's another horrible story.

女：新聞真令人沮喪。每次我打開新聞，就又有可怕的報導。

M : I know what you mean. Wars, crime, poverty—it's
endless. That's why I don't watch the news any more.

男： 我懂妳的意思。戰爭、犯罪、貧窮—說不完。那就是為什
麼我不再看新聞。

W : Well, I like to keep up with current events, so I have
no choice.

女：嗯，我想跟上時事，所以我沒選擇。

Question : Why does the woman watch the news?

女士為何看新聞？

(A) To learn more about depressing events.

要知道更多令人沮喪的事情。

(B) To keep up with current events. 要跟上時事。

(C) To help prepare for future events.

為了有助於對未來會發生的事做好準備。

* news〔njuz〕*n.* 新聞

　depressing〔dɪ'prɛsɪŋ〕*adj.* 令人沮喪的

　every time 每次；每當　　***turn on*** 打開（電器）

　horrible〔'hɔrəbl〕*adj.* 可怕的　　story〔'storɪ〕*n.* 報導

　mean〔min〕*v.* 意思是　　war〔wɔr〕*n.* 戰爭

　crime〔kraɪm〕*n.* 犯罪　　poverty〔'pɑvətɪ〕*n.* 貧窮

　endless〔'ɛndlɪs〕*adj.* 無窮盡的

　not…any more 不再…　　***keep up with*** 跟上；趕上

　current〔'kɜənt〕*adj.* 現在的　　event〔ɪ'vɛnt〕*n.* 事件

　current events 時事（= *current affairs*）

　choice〔tʃɔɪs〕*n.* 選擇　　learn〔lɜn〕*v.* 得知

　prepare〔prɪ'pɛr〕*v.* 為…而準備 < *for* >

　future〔'fjutʃə〕*adj.* 未來的

22. (**B**) M : There's been a change of plans. Mr. Walker doesn't need the sales report until Monday.

男：計畫有改變。沃克先生下週一才要銷售報告。

W : That's a relief! I sincerely doubted whether I could have it ready by Friday.

女：真是讓人鬆一口氣！我真的懷疑我是否能夠在週五前弄好報告。

M : Not to worry. You have more time. But don't wait until the last minute to get it done.

男：不用擔心。妳有更多時間。但是不要等到最後一刻才做完。

Question : What is the most likely relationship between the speakers? 說話者最可能的關係是什麼？

(A) Classmates. 同學。

(B) Colleagues. 同事。

(C) Siblings. 兄弟姊妹。

* change〔tʃendʒ〕n. 改變　　plan〔plæn〕n. 計畫
sales〔selz〕adj. 銷售的　　report〔rɪ'port〕n. 報告
relief〔rɪ'lif〕n. 放心；鬆一口氣
That's a relief! 真叫人鬆了一口氣！
sincerely〔sɪn'sɪrlɪ〕adv. 由衷地　　doubt〔daʊt〕v. 懷疑
have…ready 準備好…　　by〔baɪ〕prep. 在…之前
worry〔'wɜɪ〕v. 擔心　　**the last minute** 最後一刻；緊急時候
likely〔'laɪklɪ〕adj. 可能的
relationship〔rɪ'leʃən,ʃɪp〕n. 關係
colleague〔'kɑlig〕n. 同事（= co-worker）
siblings〔'sɪblɪŋz〕n. pl. 兄弟姊妹

23. (**C**) W : Did I hear that announcement correctly? The flight is being delayed by another hour?

女：我有聽錯剛剛的公告嗎？班機要再延遲一小時？

M : That's what it sounded like. Geez, we're already two hours past our original departure time.

男：聽起來像是那樣。唉呀，我們已經晚了原本的出發時間兩小時。

W : At this rate, we'll never get to St. Louis.

女：這樣的話，我們永遠到不了聖路易斯。

Question : Where is this conversation taking place?

這對話發生在哪裡？

(A) St. Louis. 聖路易斯。

(B) On a plane. 在飛機上。

(C) In an airport. 在機場裡。

* announcement〔əˈnaʊnsmənt〕n. 宣布;公告
  correctly〔kəˈrɛktlɪ〕adv. 正確地　　flight〔flaɪt〕n. 班機
  delay〔dɪˈle〕v. 使延誤　　**sound like** 聽起來像
  geez〔dʒiz〕interj.【表示經其、憤怒】唉呀!
  past〔pæst〕prep. 超過;過了
  original〔əˈrɪdʒənḷ〕adj. 原本的
  departure〔dɪˈpɑrtʃɚ〕n. 出發
  at this rate 這樣子;這樣的話　　**get to** 到達
  St. Louis 聖路易斯【美國密蘇里州(Missouri)的一個城市】
  conversation〔ˌkɑnvɚˈseʃən〕n. 對話
  take place 發生;出現　　plane〔plen〕n. 飛機
  airport〔ˈɛrˌport〕n. 機場

24.(**A**) W : Did you hear what Gloria said to me? I don't think
　　　　　　　　I've ever been so offended in my entire life.

　　　　女:你有聽到葛洛莉亞跟我說的話嗎?我這一生中沒這麼生氣
　　　　　　過。

　　　　M : No, I didn't hear anything, dear. What did she say?

　　　　男:不,我什麼都沒聽到,親愛的。她說了什麼?

　　　　W : Never mind, darling. I can't bear to repeat it.

　　　　女:別在意,親愛的。我無法再重複一次。

　　　　Question : How does the woman feel? 女士的感受如何?

　　　　(A) Insulted. 受侮辱的。

　　　　(B) Regretful. 後悔的。

　　　　(C) Silly. 愚蠢的。

　　　　* offend〔əˈfɛnd〕v. 冒犯;觸怒　　entire〔ɪnˈtaɪr〕adj. 全部的
　　　　　dear〔dɪr〕n. 親愛的人;愛人
　　　　　mind〔maɪnd〕v. 介意　　**Never mind.** 沒關係;別介意。
　　　　　darling〔ˈdɑrlɪŋ〕n. 親愛的人　　bear〔bɛr〕v. 忍受
　　　　　repeat〔rɪˈpit〕v. 重複　　insulted〔ɪnˈsʌltɪd〕adj. 受侮辱的
　　　　　regretful〔rɪˈgrɛtfəl〕adj. 遺憾的;後悔的
　　　　　silly〔ˈsɪlɪ〕adj. 愚蠢的

25. (**B**) M : The drama club is having a farewell party for
Professor Burns tomorrow evening.

男：戲劇社明天晚上會為彭斯教授舉辦一個告別派對。

W : Oh! I didn't know he was retiring. He's only in his
50s, isn't he?

女：喔！我不知道他要退休了。他只有五十幾歲，不是嗎？

M : He's not retiring. He took a teaching post at Oxford.

男：他不是要退休。他在牛津大學取得教職。

Question : What does the woman think about Professor
Burns? 女士對彭斯教授有什麼想法？

(A) He's not a very good actor. 他不是個很好的演員。

(B) He's too young to retire. 他太年輕，不能退休。

(C) He's very handsome. 他很英俊。

* drama〔'drɑmə〕n. 戲劇　　club〔klʌb〕n. 社團
have〔hæv〕v. 舉辦　　farewell〔ˌfɛr'wɛl〕n. 告別
professor〔prə'fɛsɚ〕n. 教授　　retire〔rɪ'taɪr〕v. 退休
post〔post〕n. 工作；職位　　*teaching post* 教職
Oxford〔'ɑksfɚd〕n. 牛津大學　　actor〔'æktɚ〕n. 男演員
too…to~ 太…而無法~　　handsome〔'hænsəm〕adj. 英俊的

26. (**A**) M : Excuse me, I'm looking for the post office.

男：很抱歉，我正在找郵局。

W : OK, keep going straight and take a right at the gas
station. You'll see the post office on the left, next to
the library.

女：好的，一直直走然後在加油站右轉。你會看到郵局在你的左
側，圖書館隔壁。

M : Thanks.

男：謝謝。

Question：What does the man most likely want to do?

男士最可能想要做什麼？

(A) Mail a package. 寄包裹。

(B) Check out a book. 借書。

(C) Fill up his gas tank. 加滿他的油箱。

* ***Excuse me***. 對不起。【用於引起對方的注意】
  look for 尋找　　***post office*** 郵局
  OK 好的；沒問題　　***keep + V-ing*** 持續
  straight〔stret〕*adv.* 直直地
  take a right 右轉（= *make a right*）
  gas station 加油站　　***on the left*** 在左側
  next to 在～隔壁　　library〔'laɪˌbrɛrɪ〕*n.* 圖書館
  likely〔'laɪklɪ〕*adv.* 可能地
  mail〔mel〕*v.* 郵寄　　package〔'pækɪdʒ〕*n.* 包裹
  check out（從圖書館）借（書）
  fill up 裝滿　　gas〔gæs〕*n.* 汽油
  tank〔tæŋk〕*n.* 槽；箱　　***gas tank***（汽車）油箱

27. (**A**) W：Hi, my name is Liz and I'll be your server tonight. Would you like to hear today's specials?

女：嗨，我的名字叫莉茲，而我今晚是你的服務人員。你想要聽聽今晚的特餐是什麼嗎？

M：No, thanks, Liz. I'm ready to order and I'm on a very tight schedule.

男：不，謝謝，莉茲。我準備好點菜了，而且我的時間很趕。

W：OK, sir. I'll make sure the kitchen is aware of that.

男：好的，先生。我會確定廚房知道到這件事。

Question：What does the man imply?

男士暗示什麼？

(A) His time is limited. 他的時間有限。

(B) His children are special. 他的孩子很特別。

(C) His pants are too tight. 他的褲子太緊。

＊server (ˋsɝvɚ) n. 服務生　　　**would like to V.** 想要～
special (ˋspɛʃəl) n. 特色菜；特餐　adj. 特別的
order (ˋɔrdɚ) v. 點菜
tight (taɪt) adj. (時間) 緊迫的；緊的
schedule (ˋskɛdʒul) n. 時間表
on a tight schedule 行程緊湊　　**make sure** 確定
kitchen (ˋkɪtʃɪn) n. 廚房　　**be aware of** 察覺到
imply (ɪmˋplaɪ) v. 暗示　　limited (ˋlɪmɪtɪd) adj. 有限的
pants (pænts) n. pl. 褲子

28. (**C**)　W : Let's get up early tomorrow morning and watch the
　　　　　　　　sunrise.

女：我們明天早起看日出吧。

　　M : Again with the sunrise idea. Haven't I already told
　　　　　you? If you've seen one, you've seen them all.

男：又是看日出的點子。我不是告訴過妳嗎？如果妳看過一
　　次，就等於看了全部。

　　W : You have no sense of wonder, Jack. Well, I'm
　　　　　waking up at dawn—you can do what you want.

女：你完全沒有好奇心，傑克。嗯，我要在破曉時起床——你
　　可以做你想做的。

　　Question : What does the woman want to do?
　　　　　　　　女士想做什麼？

(A) Watch the sunset. 看日落。

(B) Motivate the man to get more exercise.
　　激勵男士多運動。

(C) Wake up early tomorrow morning. 明天早上早起。

* *let's* + *V*. 我們一起～吧　　*get up* 起床

sunrise〔'sʌn͵raɪz〕*n.* 日出　　sense〔sɛns〕*n.* 感受

wonder〔'wʌndə〕*n.* 驚奇；驚訝

sense of wonder 驚奇感；好奇心（= *curiosity*）

sunset〔'sʌn͵sɛt〕*n.* 日落　　motivate〔'motə͵vet〕*v.* 激勵

exercise〔'ɛksə͵saɪz〕*n.* 運動　　*wake up* 醒來；起床

29. (**A**)　W：Good afternoon.　Table for one?

女：午安。一個人的座位嗎？

M：No, um, actually, I was here for dinner last night and I think I may have left my wallet at the table.

男：不，嗯，事實上，我昨晚在這裡用晚餐，我想我把我的皮夾留在桌上了。

W：You did?　Let me check with the manager to see if anyone turned in a wallet last night.

女：是嗎？讓我跟經理確定一下，是否昨晚有人撿到皮夾。

Question：What will the woman most likely do next?

女士接下來最可能做什麼？

(A) She will call the manager. 她會叫經理來。

(B) She will apologize for stealing the man's wallet.

她會因偷了男士的皮夾而道歉。

(C) She will see the man to his table.

她會帶男子到他的座位。

* um〔ʌm〕*interj.*【表示遲疑】嗯

actually〔'æktʃʊəlɪ〕*adv.* 事實上；實際上

may have + *p.p.* 過去可能～

left〔lɛft〕*v.* 遺留【leave 的過去分詞】

wallet〔'wɑlɪt〕*n.* 皮夾

check〔tʃɛk〕*v.* 檢查；洽詢 < *with* >

manager〔'mænɪdʒə〕*n.* 經理　　*turn in* 提交；歸還

likely〔'laɪklɪ〕*adv.* 可能地　　next〔nɛkst〕*adv.* 接著
call〔kɔl〕*v.* 叫；打電話給（某人）
apologize〔ə'pɑləˏdʒaɪz〕*v.* 道歉　　steal〔stil〕*v.* 偷
see〔si〕*v.* 陪同；送 < *to* >

30. (**C**) M：Ma'am, is that your dog over there? The German
　　　　　　shepherd?

男：小姐，那是妳的狗嗎？德國牧羊犬？

W：Yes, it is, officer. Why? Is there a problem?

女：是的，警察先生。怎麼了？有什麼問題嗎？

M：The dog needs to be leashed on public property.
　　I'm going to give you a warning this time, but from
　　now on…

男：狗在公用土地上需要拴起來。這一次我給妳一個警告，
　　但是從現在開始…

Question：What do we know about the dog?

　　　　　關於狗我們知道什麼？

(A) It is very playful. 牠很頑皮。

(B) It is hungy. 牠很餓。

(C) It is on public property. 牠在公用土地上。

* ma'am〔mæm〕*n.* 小姐；太太（= *madam*）
over there 在那裡　　German〔'dʒɝmən〕*adj.* 德國的
shepherd〔'ʃɛpəd〕*n.* 牧羊人
German shepherd 德國牧羊犬　　officer〔'ɔfəsə〕*n.* 警官
leash〔liʃ〕*v.* 拴住；繫住　　public〔'pʌblɪk〕*adj.* 公共的
property〔'prɑpətɪ〕*n.* 財產；地產
public property 公共財產；公用土地
warning〔'wɔrnɪŋ〕*n.* 警告　　***from now on*** 從現在開始
playful〔'plefəl〕*adj.* 愛玩的　　hungy〔'hʌŋgrɪ〕*adj.* 飢餓的

TEST 10

第一部分：辨識句意（第 1-10 題，共 10 題）

作答說明：第 1-10 題每題均有三個選項，請依據所聽到的單句，選出符合描述的圖片。

示例題：你會看到

(A)  (B) (C)

依據所播放的內容，正確答案應該選 A，請將答案紙該題「Ⓐ」的地方塗黑、塗滿，即 ●ⒷⒸ。

---

1. (A)  (B)  (C)

2. (A)  (B)  (C)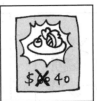

8. (A)　　　　(B)　　　　(C)

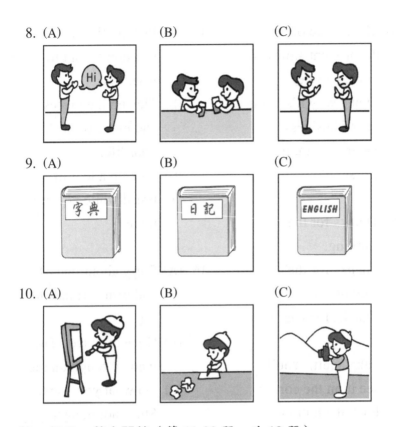

9. (A)　　　　(B)　　　　(C)

10. (A)　　　　(B)　　　　(C)

第二部分：基本問答（第 11-20 題，共 10 題）

作答說明：第 11-20 題每題均有三個選項，請依據所聽到的對話問句，選出一個最適合的回答。

示例題：你會看到

(A) She is talking to the teacher.

(B) She is a student in my class.

(C) She is wearing a beautiful dress.

依據所播放的內容，正確答案應該選 B，請將答案紙該題「Ⓑ」的地方塗黑、塗滿，即Ⓐ●Ⓒ。

11. (A) Maybe one of the department stores is having a sale.
    (B) That's why it's going out of business.
    (C) Saturdays are the worst.

12. (A) Thanks for the warning.
    (B) Thanks for the memories.
    (C) Thanks for your help.

13. (A) Take a left. You'll see it on the corner.
    (B) Push the button. The door will open briefly.
    (C) I've got a $5. Just take it and pay me back later.

14. (A) State the evidence clearly.
    (B) Tomorrow never knows.
    (C) Yes, I have.

15. (A) Pick up the pace if you don't want to lose.
    (B) Pick up the pieces and move on with your life.
    (C) Pick up a loaf of bread while you are there.

16. (A) Sorry about that. I had some errands to run.
    (B) Once or twice. They made it tough on me.
    (C) Do what you want. She's not hungry.

17. (A) Many people would have helped if they had known.
    (B) You could see it coming a mile away.
    (C) The money just isn't there.

18. (A) Check to see if it's
       plugged in.
    (B) Turn it off if you're
       not using it.
    (C) I think it's due on the
       fifth.

19. (A) Peanut butter and jelly.
    (B) Sounds good.
    (C) Have another slice.

20. (A) Cool! Finally,
       something interesting
       happens at lunch.
    (B) Darn! Why can't
       they do that for me?
    (C) Wow! I didn't know
       you had it in you.

第三部分：言談理解（第 21-30 題，共 10 題）

作答說明： 第 21-30 題每題均有三個選項，請依據所聽到的對話或短
　　　　　文內容，選出一個最適合的答案。

示例題：你會看到

(A) 9:50.　　(B) 10:00.　　(C) 10:10.

依據所播放的內容，正確答案應該選 B，請將答案紙該題「Ⓑ」
的地方塗黑、塗滿，即Ⓐ●Ⓒ。

---

21. (A) To work.
    (B) To a department store.
    (C) To a cooking class.

22. (A) In a taxi.
    (B) On a bus.
    (C) At a party.

23. (A) Replace the light bulb in the maintenance office.
    (B) Replace the light bulb in the supply closet.
    (C) Call the maintenance department.

24. (A) She is cold.
    (B) She is having trouble with her computer.
    (C) She is on her third cup of coffee.

25. (A) Excited.
    (B) Bored.
    (C) Fearful.

26. (A) Applying for a driver's license.
    (B) Getting a haircut.
    (C) Shppinging for clothing.

27. (A) Housecleaning.
    (B) Cooking.
    (C) Babysitting.

28. (A) Traffic to clear up.
    (B) Their friends to arrive.
    (C) 8:30.

29. (A) He took money from the woman's purse.
    (B) He put money in the woman's purse.
    (C) He fired the housecleaners.

30. (A) Go out to dinner.
    (B) Work late.
    (C) Throw a party.

TEST 10 詳解

第一部分：辨識句意

1. (**A**) (A)   (B)   (C)

Gary is fishing from a boat. 蓋瑞在船上釣魚。

* fish〔fɪʃ〕 *v.* 釣魚   boat〔bot〕 *n.* 船

2. (**A**) (A)   (B)   (C)

French fries are on sale for NT$25.

薯條現在特價台幣二十五元。

* *French Fries* 薯條   *on sale* 特價

3. (**B**) (A)   (B)   (C)

School lets out at three p.m.　學校下午三點放學。

　let out （學校、集會）終了；解散

　p.m. 下午（= *post meridiem* ）

4. (**B**) (A)　　　　　　(B)　　　　　　(C)

You can see the mountain through the open window.
你可以透過敞開的窗戶看到山。

　* window〔ˈwɪndo〕*n.* 窗戶

5. (**C**) (A)　　　　　　(B)　　　　　　(C)

The box won't fit in the mailbox.　箱子無法放進郵筒。

　* box〔baks〕*n.* 箱子；盒子　　*fit in* 放進去；裝入
　mailbox〔ˈmel,baks〕*n.* 郵筒

6. (**C**) (A)　　　　　　(B)　　　　　　(C)

Henry is full.　亨利吃飽了。

　* full〔fʊl〕*adj.* 飽的

7. (**B**) (A)  (B) 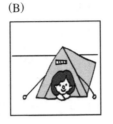 (C)

Selina is camping. 賽琳娜在露營。

* camp〔kæmp〕*v.* 露營

8. (**C**) (A)  (B)  (C)

Tim and Tom can never agree on anything.

提姆和湯姆意見從未一致。

* agree〔ə'gri〕*v.* 同意；意見一致

   agree on sth. 對某事意見一致

9. (**C**) (A)  (B) 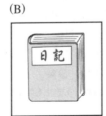 (C)

English is my best subject. 英文是我最好的科目。

* subject〔'sʌbdʒɪkt〕*n.* 科目

10. (**A**) (A) (B) (C)

Peter is a painter. 彼得是個畫家。

* painter〔'pentɚ〕 *n.* 畫家

第二部分：基本問答

11. (**A**) The mall is so crowded! I wonder why there are so many people here on a Tuesday.

購物中心好擁擠！我在想為什麼星期二這裡會有這麼多人。

(A) Maybe one of the department stores is having a sale.

或許其中一家百貨公司正大拍賣。

(B) That's why it's going out of business.

那就是為什麼它快要倒閉了。

(C) Saturdays are the worst. 週六是最糟的。

* mall〔mɔl〕 *n.* 購物中心
crowded〔'kraʊdɪd〕 *adj.* 擁擠的
wonder〔'wʌndɚ〕 *v.* 想知道
maybe〔'mebi〕 *adv.* 可能；或許
department store 百貨公司　　sale〔sel〕 *n.* 拍賣
business〔'bɪznɪs〕 *n.* 營業
go out of business 停業；倒閉

12. (**A**) Be careful what you say around Ms. Smith today. She's not in a good mood.

今天在史密斯小姐旁邊說話要小心。她心情不好。

(A) Thanks for the warning. 謝謝你警告我。

(B) Thanks for the memories. 謝謝你給我的回憶。

(C) Thanks for your help. 謝謝你的幫忙。

* careful〔'kɛrfəl〕*adj.* 小心的　　mood〔mud〕*n.* 心情
  be in a good mood 心情好　　warning〔'wɔrnɪŋ〕*n.* 警告
  help〔hɛlp〕*n.* 幫忙

13. (**C**) Do you have change for a $20? I need to tip the waiter.
    你有二十塊的零錢嗎？我需要小費給服務生。

    (A) Take a left. You'll see it on the corner.
    左轉。你會看到它就在轉角。

    (B) Push the button. The door will open briefly.
    按下按鈕。門會打開一下子。

    (C) I've got a $5. Just take it and pay me back later.
    我有五塊錢。就拿去吧，待會再還我。

    * change〔tʃendʒ〕*n.* 零錢　　tip〔tɪp〕*v.* 給…小費
      waiter〔'wetɚ〕*n.* 服務生
      corner〔'kɔrnɚ〕*n.* 角落；轉角　　push〔puʃ〕*v.* 推；按
      button〔'bʌtn̩〕*n.* 按鈕　　briefly〔'briflɪ〕*adv.* 短暫地
      pay back 償還　　later〔'letɚ〕*adv.* 待會

14. (**C**) The final exam is tomorrow. I assume you've been
    studying. 期末考是明天。我想你一直有在讀書。

    (A) State the evidence clearly. 清楚說明證據。

    (B) Tomorrow never knows. 無人能預知明天。【詳見背景說明】

    (C) Yes, I have. 是的，我有。

    * exam〔ɪg'zæm〕*n.* 考試（＝*examination*）
      assume〔ə'sum〕*n.* 假定；認為
      state〔stet〕*v.* 陳述；說明　　evidence〔'ɛvədəns〕*n.* 證據
      clearly〔'klɪrlɪ〕*adv.* 清楚地

15. (**C**) Oh, and I'll stop by the supermarket on the way home. We're out of milk.

喔，我回家途中會順道去超市一趟。我們沒牛奶了。

(A) Pick up the pace if you don't want to lose.

要加快速度，如果你不想輸的話。

(B) Pick up the pieces and move on with your life.

收拾殘局，然後繼續過你的生活。

(C) Pick up a loaf of bread while you are there.

當你在那裡的時候，買一條麵包。

* ***stop by*** 順道去；順道拜訪

supermarket ('supɚ͵markɪt) *n.* 超級市場

on the way 往…的路上　　***be out of*** 用完…

pick up 加快　　pace (pes) *n.* 步伐；速度

lose (luz) *v.* 失去；輸掉　　piece (pis) *n.* 一片

pick up the pieces 收拾殘局；恢復正常

move on 繼續前進　　loaf (lof) *n.* 一條 (麵包)

bread (brɛd) *n.* 麵包　　while (hwaɪl) *conj.* 當…的時候

16. (**A**) There you are, Wilson. We missed you at lunch this afternoon.

你終於來了，威爾森。今天下午我們吃午餐時很想你。

(A) Sorry about that. I had some errands to run.

很抱歉。我有些事要辦。

(B) Once or twice. They made it tough on me.

一次或兩次。他們刁難我。

(C) Do what you want. She's not hungry.

做你想做的。她不餓。

* ***There you are***. 你終於來了。

errand ('ɛrənd) *n.* 事情；差事　　***run an errand*** 跑腿；辦事

once (wʌns) *adv.* 一次　　twice (twaɪs) *adv.* 兩次

tough (tʌf) *adj.* 費力的；困難的

be tough on 對…嚴厲；刁難…

17. (**B**) The movie was OK but the ending was predictable and disappointing. 電影還可以，但是結局預測得到且讓人失望。

(A) Many people would have helped if they had known.
很多人會幫忙，如果他們知道的話。

(B) You could see it coming a mile away.
你可以預測到結局。【詳見背景說明】

(C) The money just isn't there. 我們沒有錢。【詳見背景說明】

* ending〔'ɛndɪŋ〕*n.* 結局
predictable〔prɪ'dɪktəbļ〕*adj.* 可預測的
disappointing〔,dɪsə'pɔɪntɪŋ〕*adj.* 令人失望的
see sth. coming (a mile away) 知道某事正要發生
mile〔maɪl〕*n.* 哩；英里【一英里等於 1.6093 公里】

18. (**C**) Honey, I can't find the electric bill. Do you remember when it's due?
親愛的，我找不到電費帳單。你記得幾號到期嗎？

(A) Check to see if it's plugged in.
看看插頭有沒有插進去。

(B) Turn it off if you're not using it.
如果你沒在使用，就關掉。

(C) I think it's due on the fifth. 我想是在五號到期。

* honey〔'hʌnɪ〕*n.*【暱稱】親愛的
electric〔ɪ'lɛktrɪk〕*adj.* 電的　　bill〔bɪl〕*n.* 帳單
due〔dju〕*adj.* 到期的　　check〔tʃɛk〕*v.* 檢查
plug〔plʌg〕*v.* 給…接通電源 < *in* >
turn off 關掉（電器）　　use〔juz〕*v.* 使用

19. (**B**) I'm starving. Let's order a pizza.
我快餓死了。我們點披薩吧。

(A) Peanut butter and jelly. 花生醬跟果凍。

(B) Sounds good. 聽起來不錯。

(C) Have another slice. 再吃一片。

* starve〔 stɑrv 〕*v.* 餓
　　　　let's + V. 我們一起~吧
　　　　order〔ˈɔrdə〕*v.* 訂購；點（餐）　　pizza〔ˈpitsə〕*n.* 披薩
　　　　peanut〔ˈpiˌnʌt〕*n.* 花生　　butter〔ˈbʌtə〕*n.* 奶油；醬
　　　　jelly〔ˈdʒɛlɪ〕*n.* 果凍　　sound〔 saʊnd 〕*v.* 聽起來
　　　　have〔 hæv 〕*v.* 吃　　slice〔 slaɪs 〕*n.* 一片

20.(**A**) Uh-oh, something's going on over there. Looks like a
　　　　fight! 呃喔，那裡有事發生了。看起來像是打架！

　　(A) Cool! Finally, something interesting happens at lunch.
　　　　好酷喔！終於有有趣的事情在午餐時候發生。

　　(B) Darn! Why can't they do that for me?
　　　　真該死！他們為什麼不幫我做？

　　(C) Wow! I didn't know you had it in you.
　　　　哇！我不知道你深藏不露。

　　　　* uh-oh〔ˈʌˌo〕*interj.* 【表示驚訝、不安等】呃喔
　　　　go on 發生　　***over there*** 在那裡
　　　　look〔 lʊk 〕*v.* 看起來　　fight〔 faɪt 〕*n.* 打架
　　　　cool〔 kul 〕*adj.* 很酷的
　　　　finally〔ˈfaɪnḷɪ〕*adv.* 最後；終於
　　　　interesting〔ˈɪntrɪstɪŋ〕*adj.* 有趣的
　　　　darn〔 dɑrn 〕*interj.* 真該死（= *damn*）
　　　　have it in *sb.* 有能力（做某事）；深藏不露【詳見背景說明】

第三部分：言談理解

21.(**B**) M：Where are you going with the new microwave?
　　　　男：妳要帶著新的微波爐去哪？

　　　　W：It's not working. I'm exchanging it for a new one.
　　　　女：它不動了。我要換一台新的。

　　　　M：Here, let me help you. It's much too heavy for one
　　　　　　person to carry.
　　　　男：嘿，讓我幫妳。一個人拿太重了。

Question：Where is the woman most likely going?

　　　　　女士最可能要去哪裡？

(A) To work. 去上班。

(B) To a department store. 去百貨公司。

(C) To a cooking class. 去烹飪課。

＊ microwave (ˈmaɪkrəˌwev) n. 微波爐 (= microwave oven)
work (wɜk) v. 運轉　　exchange (ɪksˈtʃendʒ) v. 退換
here (hɪr) interj. 嘿！　　carry (ˈkærɪ) v. 搬運
likely (ˈlaɪklɪ) adv. 可能地　　department store 百貨公司
cooking (ˈkʊkɪŋ) adj. 烹飪的　　class (klæs) n. 課程

22. (**C**) W：You're not leaving the party so soon, are you, Ted?
Let me call you a taxi.

女：你沒有那麼快就離開派對，泰德，是吧？讓我幫你叫台計
程車。

M：I'm fine. I can drive myself.

男：我沒事。我可以自己開車。

W：That's not a good idea. You're in no condition to drive.

女：那不是個好主意。你的狀況不適合開車。

Question：Where is this conversation taking place?

　　　　　這對話出現在哪裡？

(A) In a taxi. 在計程車上。

(B) On a bus. 在公車上。

(C) At a party. 在派對上。

＊ drive (draɪv) v. 開車　　condition (kənˈdɪʃən) n. 狀況
be in no condition to V. (身體狀況) 不適合做～
conversation (ˌkɑnvəˈseʃən) n. 對話　　**take place** 發生

23. (**C**) W：The light bulb is burned out in the supply closet.

女：儲藏櫃裡的燈泡燒壞了。

M : Did you call someone from maintenance to have
    them replace it?

男：妳有打電話給維修部的人來換嗎？

W : No. I guess I should do that, shouldn't I?

女：沒有。我想那是我應該做的，不是嗎？

Question : What will the woman most likely do next?

　　　　女士接下來最可能做什麼？

(A) Replace the light bulb in the maintenance office.
    更換維修部的燈泡。

(B) Replace the light bulb in the supply closet.
    更換儲藏櫃的燈泡。

(C) Call the maintenance department.
    打電話給維修部門。

* bulb〔bʌlb〕*n.* 燈泡　　　***light bulb*** 燈泡
  burn out 燒光；燒壞　　supply〔sə'plaɪ〕*n.* 供應
  closet〔'klɑzɪt〕*n.* 櫥櫃　　***supply closet*** 儲藏櫃
  maintenance〔'mentənəns〕*n.* 維修
  replace〔rɪ'ples〕*v.* 更換　　guess〔gɛs〕*v.* 推測；認為
  office〔'ɔfɪs〕*n.* 辦公室；…部
  department〔dɪ'pɑrtmənt〕*n.* 部門

24. (**B**) M : Have you had your coffee break yet?

　　　　　男：妳已經休息喝過咖啡了嗎？

　　　　W : Not yet. My computer keeps freezing up, and I can't
　　　　　　close these files.

　　　　女：還沒。我的電腦一直當機，而我無法把這些檔案關閉。

　　　　M : Oh, maybe I can help. Let me take a look at it.

　　　　男：喔，或許我可以幫忙。讓我看一下。

　　　　Question : What is the woman's problem?

　　　　　　　　　女士有什麼問題？

　　　　(A) She is cold. 她很冷。

(B) She is having trouble with her computer.

她的電腦有問題。

(C) She is on her third cup of coffee.

她在喝她的第三杯咖啡。

* break〔brek〕*n.* 休息時間

coffee break 喝咖啡休息時間　　*not yet* 尚未；還沒

freeze〔friz〕*v.* 結冰；（電腦）當機

freeze up （電腦）當機；停止運轉

file〔faɪl〕*n.* 檔案　　*take a look at* 看一下

have trouble with 有問題　　on〔ɑn〕*prep.* 服用；吃

25. (**A**) M：The show should start any minute now. I can't wait!

男：表演應該很快就開始。我等不及了！

W：Me too! I'm so excited. It's my first time seeing the band.

女：我也是！我好興奮。這是我第一次看這樂團。

M：Really? Well, I hope they play all of their big hits.

男：眞的嗎？嗯，我希望他們會演奏他們所有的熱門歌曲。

Question：How does the woman feel?

女士的感覺如何？

(A) Excited. 興奮的。

(B) Bored. 無聊的。

(C) Fearful. 害怕的。

* show〔ʃo〕*n.* 表演　　*any minute* 隨時（ = *very soon* ）

can't wait 等不及　　excited〔ɪkˈsaɪtɪd〕*adj.* 興奮的

band〔bænd〕*n.* 樂團　　play〔ple〕*v.* 演奏

hit〔hɪt〕*n.* 受歡迎的事物；熱門歌曲

bored〔bord〕*adj.* 無聊的

fearful〔ˈfɪrfəl〕*adj.* 害怕的

26. (**A**) W：When you've completed the application, bring it to window number 5.

女：當你寫完申請書，就把這拿到五號窗口。

M：Will I need to provide identification?

男：我需要提供身份證明嗎？

W：You will have to show two forms of ID. Passports, birth certificates, student IDs, and Social Security cards are acceptable.

女：你必須出示兩種身份證明。護照、出生證明、學生證，和社會安全卡都可接受。

Question：What is the man probably doing?

男士可能在做什麼？

(A) Applying for a driver's license. 申請駕照。

(B) Getting a haircut. 剪頭髮。

(C) Shppinging for clothing. 買衣服。

* complete〔kəm'plit〕*v.* 完成

application〔ˌæplə'keʃən〕*n.* 申請書

provide〔prə'vaɪd〕*v.* 提供

identification〔aɪˌdɛntəfə'keʃən〕*n.* 身份證明（= ID）

show〔ʃo〕*v.* 出示

form〔form〕*n.* 形式；種類

passport〔'pæsˌport〕*n.* 護照

certificate〔sə'tɪfəkɪt〕*n.* 證明書

birth certificate 出生證明　　***student ID*** 學生證

social〔'soʃəl〕*adj.* 社會的　　security〔sə'kjurətɪ〕*n.* 安全

Social Security card 社會安全卡【新移民抵達美國後，首先要向所屬城市或鄰近地區的社會安全局（Social Security Administration）申請一張社會安全卡，俗稱「工卡」。卡上登記著社會安全卡持有人的姓名及一個九位數的「社會安全號碼」（Social Security Number）】

acceptable〔ək'sɛptəbḷ〕*adj.* 可接受的

apply〔ə'plaɪ〕*v.* 申請 *< for >*
license〔'laɪsn̩s〕*n.* 執照
driver's license 駕駛執照
haircut〔'hɛr,kʌt〕*n.* 理髮　　***shop for*** 購買 (= *buy*)
clothing〔'kloðɪŋ〕*n.*【總稱】衣服

27. (**C**)　W：Thanks for coming to watch the kids on such short
　　　　　　notice, Rod. If you get hungry, there's leftover fried
　　　　　　chicken in the fridge.

　　　女：謝謝你這麼臨時來看管孩子，羅德。如果你餓了，冰箱裡有
　　　　　吃剩的炸雞。

　　　M：Thanks, Marge. I may help myself to a piece or two.

　　　男：謝謝，瑪姬。我會自己吃個一兩塊。

　　　W：OK, you have my cell phone number. Call if there's
　　　　　an emergency.

　　　女：好的，你有我的手機號碼。如果有緊急事故，打電話給我。

　　　Question：What is Rod doing? 羅德在做什麼？

　　　(A) Housecleaning. 大掃除。

　　　(B) Cooking. 煮飯。

　　　(C) Babysitting. 當臨時保姆。

　　* ***thanks for*** 謝謝你…　　　watch〔wɑtʃ〕*v.* 看護；照顧
　　　notice〔'notɪs〕*n.* 通知
　　　on short notice 一收到通知就…；臨時
　　　hungry〔'hʌŋgrɪ〕*adj.* 飢餓的
　　　leftover〔'lɛft,ovɚ〕*adj.* 剩下的；吃剩的
　　　fried chicken 炸雞　　　fridge〔frɪdʒ〕*n.* 冰箱
　　　help *oneself* ***to*** 自行取用　　　***cell phone*** 手機
　　　emergency〔ɪ'mɝdʒənsɪ〕*n.* 緊急情況
　　　housecleaning〔'haʊs,klinɪŋ〕*n.* 大掃除
　　　babysit〔'bebɪ,sɪt〕*v.* 擔任臨時保姆

28. (**B**) M : The Jensens are late again. I don't know why I ever expect them to show up on time. They never do.

　　　男：詹森一家人又遲到了。我不知爲何我會期待他們準時出現。他們從來沒準時過。

　　　W : Oh, come on, Dick. They're coming all the way down from Milwaukee. Traffic could be bad, too.

　　　女：喔，算了吧，迪克。他們大老遠從密爾瓦基市過來。交通狀況也可能很糟糕。

　　　M : If you tell someone you'll be there by 8:30, you should figure out a way to be there by 8:30.

　　　男：如果你跟別人說你會在八點三十分前到，你應該想辦法在八點三十分前抵達。

　　　Question : What are the speakers waiting for?

　　　　　　　說話者在等什麼？

　　　(A) Traffic to clear up. 交通暢通。

　　　(B) Their friends to arrive. 他們的朋友到來。

　　　(C) 8:30. 八點三十分。

＊ expect〔ɪk'spɛkt〕v. 預期；期待
　　show up 出現
　　on time 準時　　***come on*** 好啦；算了啦
　　all the way 一路上；老遠地
　　Milwaukee〔mɪl'wɔkɪ〕n. 密爾瓦基市【位於美國威斯康辛州】
　　traffic〔'træfɪk〕n. 交通
　　by〔baɪ〕prep. 在…之前
　　figure out 解決；想出
　　way〔we〕n. 方法
　　clear up （交通）暢通
　　arrive〔ə'raɪv〕v. 到達

29. (**A**) W : James.　There's some money missing from my purse.
　　　　　Do you know anything about it?

　　女：詹姆士。我錢包裡有些錢不見了。你知道些什麼嗎？

　　　　M : I'm sorry, Debbie.　I used $50 to pay the
　　　　　housecleaners.　I should have told you.

　　男：我很抱歉，黛比。我用了五十元付給房屋打掃工。我應該
　　　　跟妳說的。

　　　　W : That's OK.　I'm actually relieved since I thought
　　　　　one of the kids took it.

　　女：沒關係。事實上我鬆了一口氣，因為我以為是孩子拿了錢。

　　　　Question : What did the man do?

　　　　　　　　　男士做了什麼？

　　(A) He took money from the woman's purse.

　　　　他拿了女士錢包裡的錢。

　　(B) He put money in the woman's purse.

　　　　他把錢放在女士的錢包裡。

　　(C) He fired the housecleaners.

　　　　他解雇了房屋打掃工。

　　* missing〔'mɪsɪŋ〕*adj.* 不見的
　　　purse〔pɝs〕*n.* 錢包
　　　pay〔pe〕*v.* 付錢給
　　　housecleaner〔'haʊs,klinɚ〕*n.* 打掃房屋者
　　　should have + p.p. 早該～
　　　actually〔'æktʃʊəlɪ〕*adv.* 事實上；實際上
　　　relieved〔rɪ'livd〕*adj.* 放心的；鬆了一口氣的
　　　since〔sɪns〕*conj.* 因為
　　　fire〔faɪr〕*v.* 解雇；開除

30. (**B**)　M : I'll be working late tonight, Marcy, so I'll probably
　　　　　　　miss out on dinner. But I'm still coming to the party.

　　　　男：我今晚會工作到很晚，瑪西，所以我可能會錯過晚餐。
　　　　　　但我還是會去派對。

　　　　W : No problem, Richard. We have so much food; there's
　　　　　　no chance we can eat it all. I'll save you a plate.

　　　　女：沒關係，理查。我們有很多食物，不可能全部吃完。我會
　　　　　　幫你留一盤。

　　　　M : That's very thoughtful of you. I should be there
　　　　　　around ten.

　　　　男：妳真體貼。我應該十點左右會到那裡。

　　　Question : What will the man do tonight?

　　　　　　　　男士今晚要做什麼？

(A) Go out to dinner. 去外面吃晚餐。

(B) Work late. 工作到很晚。

(C) Throw a party. 舉辦派對。

* late〔let〕adv. 晚地；到很晚
　probably〔'prɑbəblɪ〕adv. 可能　　**miss out on** 錯過
　No problem. 沒關係。
　chance〔tʃæns〕n. 機會；可能性
　save〔sev〕v. 留…給（某人）
　thoughtful〔'θɔtfəl〕adj. 體貼的
　around〔ə'raʊnd〕prep. 大約（= about）
　throw〔θro〕v. 舉辦

TEST 11

第一部分：辨識句意（第 1-10 題，共 10 題）

作答說明：第 1-10 題每題均有三個選項，請依據所聽到的單句，選出符合描述的圖片。

示例題：你會看到

(A)   (B)   (C)

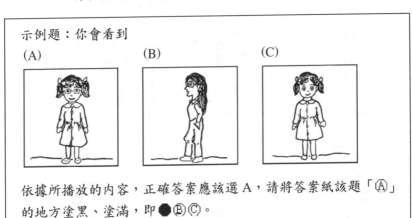

依據所播放的內容，正確答案應該選 A，請將答案紙該題「Ⓐ」的地方塗黑、塗滿，即 ●ⒷⒸ。

1. (A)   (B)   (C)

2. (A)   (B)   (C)

3. (A)　　　　　　(B)　　　　　　(C)

4. (A)　　　　　　(B)　　　　　　(C)

5. (A)　　　　　　(B)　　　　　　(C)

6. (A)　　　　　　(B)　　　　　　(C)

7. (A)　　　　　　(B)　　　　　　(C)

8. (A)　　　　(B)　　　　(C)

9. (A)　　　　(B)　　　　(C)

10. (A)　　　　(B)　　　　(C)

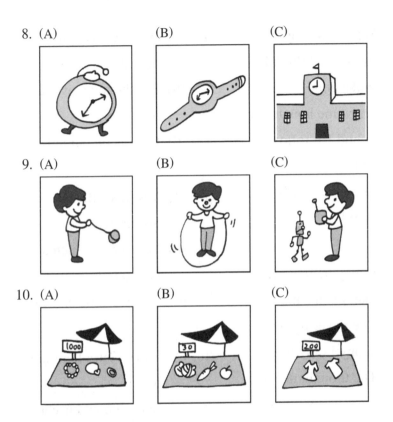

第二部分：基本問答（第 11-20 題，共 10 題）

作答說明： 第 11-20 題每題均有三個選項，請依據所聽到的對話問句，選出一個最適合的回答。

示例題：你會看到

(A) She is talking to the teacher.

(B) She is a student in my class.

(C) She is wearing a beautiful dress.

依據所播放的內容，正確答案應該選 B，請將答案紙該題「Ⓑ」的地方塗黑、塗滿，即Ⓐ●Ⓒ。

11. (A) What's wrong with my suit? I think it looks good.

(B) Show me how to do it, and I'll follow suit.

(C) The music suits the mood.

12. (A) It may be more fun than I can handle.

(B) I've never been so happy in my life.

(C) The thought never crossed my mind.

13. (A) Let's have a talk with his teacher.

(B) Let's have a talk with his coach.

(C) Let's have a talk with his pastor.

14. (A) Well, we gave it our best shot.

(B) I'm the toughest guy in school.

(C) Luck is on our side.

15. (A) Yes, it's better in Springfield.

(B) Yes, they're such a nice family.

(C) Yes, we'll be on time.

16. (A) Sorry. Turn the light on.

(B) Sure. I could use a break.

(C) Always. Never a dull moment.

17. (A) Have I been to Tokyo?

(B) Jane is kind of pushy, isn't she?

(C) That depends on what they want to do.

18. (A) You're right. I've been on a diet.
    (B) You're wrong. I've been here the whole time.
    (C) You're late. I've been here over an hour.

19. (A) That sounds like a problem.
    (B) Winning isn't everything.
    (C) With knives.

20. (A) Fried chicken.
    (B) The driver doesn't carry exact change.
    (C) The idea has become less important.

第三部分：言談理解（第 21-30 題，共 10 題）

作答説明： 第 21-30 題每題均有三個選項，請依據所聽到的對話或短文內容，選出一個最適合的答案。

示例題：你會看到

(A) 9:50.　　(B) 10:00.　　(C) 10:10.

依據所播放的內容，正確答案應該選 B，請將答案紙該題「Ⓑ」的地方塗黑、塗滿，即Ⓐ●Ⓒ。

21. (A) A new job.
    (B) A new friend.
    (C) A new place to live.

22. (A) City Hall.
    (B) The library.
    (C) The train station.

23. (A) It's too expensive.
    (B) It's too big.
    (C) It's the wrong color.

24. (A) She has an eating disorder.
    (B) She has a brain tumor.
    (C) She has breast cancer.

25. (A) He also wants to see a movie tonight.
    (B) He doesn't pay much attention to movies.
    (C) He is jealous of his brother's knowledge.

26. (A) A love letter.
    (B) An epic poem.
    (C) A short story.

27. (A) Teacher–student.
    (B) Mother–son.
    (C) Father–daughter.

28. (A) Air mail is too expensive.
    (B) Air mail is not fast enough.
    (C) Air mail is the best option.

29. (A) The woman's weight loss program.
    (B) The man's watch.
    (C) The stranger's attitude.

30. (A) They have pale skin that burns easily.
    (B) They are taking a day off from work.
    (C) They will spend the next week at the beach.

TEST 11 詳解

第一部分:辨識句意

1. (**C**) (A)   (B)   (C)

Peter has a pet rabbit. 彼得有一隻寵物兔。

* pet〔pɛt〕*n.* 寵物   *adj.*(作)寵物的
    rabbit〔'ræbɪt〕*n.* 兔子

2. (**B**) (A)   (B)   (C)

We live in an apartment building. 我們住在一棟公寓大樓。

* apartment〔ə'pɑrtmənt〕*n.* 公寓
    building〔'bɪldɪŋ〕*n.* 建築物;大樓
    apartment building 公寓大樓

3. (**A**) (A)   (B)   (C)

Linda's purse is shaped like a triangle.

琳達的錢包形狀像是個三角形。

* purse〔pɝs〕n. 錢包　　shaped〔ʃept〕adj. 有…形狀的
　triangle〔'traɪ‚æŋgḷ〕n. 三角形

4. (**A**) (A)　　　　　　(B)　　　　　　(C)

Victoria enjoys walking in the rain.

維多利亞喜歡在雨中散步。

* **enjoy + V-ing** 喜歡~　　walk〔wɔk〕v. 走路；散步

5. (**B**) (A)　　　　　　(B)　　　　　　(C)

I'll give you NT$100 to stop talking.

我會給你台幣一百元，請你停止說話。

* **stop + V-ing** 停止~

6. (**C**) (A)　　　　　　(B)　　　　　　(C)

Will you attend the Dragon Boat Festival with us?

你要跟我們一起慶祝端午節嗎？

* attend〔ə'tɛnd〕v. 參加；出席　　dragon〔'drægən〕n. 龍
boat〔bot〕n. 船　　festival〔'fɛstəvl̩〕n. 節日；慶典
the Dragon Boat Festival 端午節

7. (**C**) (A)　　　　　　(B)　　　　　　(C)

I hate washing dishes.　我討厭洗碗盤。

* hate〔het〕v. 討厭　　dishes〔'dɪʃɪz〕n. pl. 碗盤

8. (**C**) (A)　　　　　　(B)　　　　　　(C)

It's nine o'clock in the morning.　現在是早上九點。

* o'clock〔ə'klɑk〕adv. …點鐘

9. (**A**) (A)　　　　　　(B)　　　　　　(C)

William is playing with a yo-yo.　威廉在玩溜溜球。

* yo-yo〔'jo,jo〕n. 溜溜球

10. (**A**) (A)   (B)   (C)

The jewelry is on sale. 珠寶在特價。

* jewelry〔'dʒuəlrɪ〕*n.*【集合名詞】珠寶

  on sale 拍賣中；特價中

第二部分：基本問答

11. (**A**) You're not wearing that wrinkled old suit to the party, are you? 你不會穿那件又皺又舊的西裝去派對吧，是嗎？

  (A) What's wrong with my suit? I think it looks good.

     我的西裝有什麼問題嗎？我覺得看起來很好。

  (B) Show me how to do it, and I'll follow suit.

     告訴我要怎麼做，我會照做。

  (C) The music suits the mood. 音樂很適合現在的心情。

* wear〔wɛr〕*v.* 穿著

  wrinkled〔'rɪŋkld〕*adj.* 有皺紋的；皺的

  suit〔sut〕*n.* 西裝 *v.* 適合

  What's wrong with? …有什麼問題？

  look〔lʊk〕*v.* 看起來

  show〔ʃo〕*v.* 給（某人）看；告訴（某人）怎麼做

  follow〔'falo〕*v.* 遵循   ***follow suit*** 照著做

  mood〔mud〕*n.* 心情

12. (**A**) If you're not busy this weekend, would you mind helping me paint my living room?

如果你這個週末不忙，你介意幫我油漆我的客廳嗎？

  (A) It may be more fun than I can handle.

     這可能比我能做的還有趣。

(B) I've never been so happy in my life.
我一生中沒這麼高興過。

(C) The thought never crossed my mind.
我從沒有過這種想法。

* busy〔'bɪzɪ〕*adj.* 忙的　　***mind + V-ing*** 介意～
paint〔pent〕*v.* 油漆　　***living room*** 客廳
handle〔'hændḷ〕*v.* 應付；處理　　thought〔θɔt〕*n.* 想法
cross〔krɔs〕*v.* 越過；(想法)浮現(心頭)
cross one's mind 某人突然想到

13. (**A**) I'm concerned about Ricky. His grades aren't improving.
我很關心瑞奇。他的成績沒有進步。

(A) Let's have a talk with his teacher.
我們來跟他的老師談一下。

(B) Let's have a talk with his coach.
我們來跟他的教練談一下。

(C) Let's have a talk with his pastor.
我們來跟他的牧師談一下。

* concerned〔kən'sɜnd〕*adj.* 擔心的；關心的
grade〔gred〕*n.* 成績；分數　　improve〔ɪm'pruv〕*v.* 進步
let's + V. 我們一起～吧
have a talk with 與…談話　　coach〔kotʃ〕*n.* 教練
pastor〔'pæstɚ〕*n.* 牧師

14. (**A**) Bad luck last night. You can't win them all.
昨晚真不幸。你無法打敗他們全部。

(A) Well, we gave it our best shot.
嗯，我們已經盡力。

(B) I'm the toughest guy in school.
我是學校裡最頑強的人。

(C) Luck is on our side. 幸運之神在我們這邊。

* ***bad luck*** 不幸   win〔wɪn〕*v.* 戰勝；打贏
    shot〔ʃɑt〕*n.* 嘗試   ***give it*** *one's* ***best shot*** 盡全力
    guy〔gaɪ〕*n.* 人；傢伙
    on *one's* ***side*** 站在某人的一邊；支持某人
    Luck is on our side. 幸運之神在我們這邊。
     (= *Luck is with us.*)

15. (**B**) The Browns are moving to Springfield. It will be sad to
         see them go.
         布朗一家人要搬到斯普林菲爾德。要看著他們離開會很難過。

      (A) Yes, it's better in Springfield.
         是的，在斯普林菲爾德比較好。
      (B) Yes, they're such a nice family.
         是的，他們一家人真的很好。
      (C) Yes, we'll be on time. 是的，我們會準時。

    * move〔muv〕*v.* 搬家
    Springfield〔'sprɪŋ,fild〕*n.* 斯普林菲爾德【美國伊利諾伊州首府】
    on time 準時

16. (**B**) We're going down to grab a cup of coffee. Care to join
         us? 我們要去附近喝杯咖啡。想要加入我們嗎？

      (A) Sorry. Turn the light on. 抱歉。把燈打開。
      (B) Sure. I could use a break.
         當然。我很想要休息一下。
      (C) Always. Never a dull moment.
         總是如此。從來沒有無聊的一刻。

    * down〔daʊn〕*adv.* 在附近；到附近
    grab〔græb〕*v.* 抓；趕緊（吃東西等）
    care to V. 想要～   join〔dʒɔɪn〕*v.* 加入
    turn on 打開（電器）
    could use 很想要（ = *need sth. very much* ）
    break〔brek〕*n.* 休息時間   dull〔dʌl〕*adj.* 無聊的
    moment〔'momənt〕*n.* 片刻；一會兒

17. (**C**) Jane and her friends are going to Tokyo. Do you have any suggestions for them?

珍和她的朋友要去東京。你有什麼建議要給她們嗎？

(A) Have I been to Tokyo? 我去過東京嗎？

(B) Jane is kind of pushy, isn't she?

珍有點強勢，不是嗎？

(C) That depends on what they want to do.

那要看她們想要做什麼。

* Tokyo ('tokɪ,o) *n.* 東京【日本首都】
suggestion (səg'dʒɛstʃən) *n.* 建議　***have been to*** 去過
kind of 有點　　pushy ('puʃɪ) *adj.* 強勢的
depend (dɪ'pɛnd) *v.* 依靠；視…而定
depend on 取決於；視～而定

18. (**A**) You look like you've lost some weight, Steve.

你看起來好像減輕了一些體重，史帝夫。

(A) You're right. I've been on a diet.

你說得對。我在節食。

(B) You're wrong. I've been here the whole time.

你錯了。我一直在這裡。

(C) You're late. I've been here over an hour.

你遲到了。我在這裡超過一小時了。

* lost (lɔst) *v.* 失去【三態為：lose-lost-lost】
weight (wet) *n.* 體重　　***lose weight*** 減重
You're right. 你說得對。　diet ('daɪət) *n.* 節食
be on a diet 節食中　　whole (hol) *adj.* 整整的

19. (**A**) Bobby is very unpopular at school. He has made many enemies. 巴比在學校非常不受歡迎。他已經樹立了很多敵人。

(A) That sounds like a problem. 那聽起來是個問題。

(B) Winning isn't everything. 勝利不是一切。

(C) With knives. 用刀子。

* unpopular〔ʌn'pɑpjələ〕*adj.* 不受歡迎的
    enemy〔'ɛnəmɪ〕*n.* 敵人　　***sound like*** 聽起來像
    win〔wɪn〕*v.* 獲勝　　knives〔naɪvz〕*n.* 刀子【knife 的複數】

20. (**A**)　I think I'm going to have the pasta. What about you?
    我想我要吃義大利。你呢？

    (A) Fried chicken. 炸雞。

    (B) The driver doesn't carry exact change.
        司機沒有帶剛好的零錢。

    (C) The idea has become less important.
        那點子已經變得比較不重要。

    * pasta〔'pɑstə〕*n.* 義大利麵　　***What about you?*** 你呢？
    fried〔fraɪd〕*adj.* 油煎的；油炸的　　chicken〔'tʃɪkən〕*n.* 雞
    driver〔'draɪvə〕*n.* 司機　　carry〔'kærɪ〕*v.* 攜帶
    exact〔ɪg'zækt〕*adj.* 恰好的　　change〔tʃendʒ〕*n.* 零錢
    important〔ɪm'pɔrtənt〕*adj.* 重要的

第三部分：言談理解

21. (**C**)　W : I'm looking for a new apartment. Have you any
            leads for me?

    女：我在找一間新公寓。你有什麼線索嗎？

    M : Yes, actually. There's a one-bedroom for rent in the
        building across the street from my place.

    男：事實上，有的。我住的地方的對面大樓有個房間要出租。

    W : Great. Thanks for the tip. I'll check it out.

    女：太棒了。謝謝你的情報。我會去看看。

    Question : What is the woman looking for?
            女士在找什麼？

    (A) A new job. 一個新工作。

    (B) A new friend. 一位新朋友。

    (C) A new place to live. 一個新的住所。

* *look for* 尋找　　apartment〔ə'partmənt〕*n.* 公寓
Have you any~? 你有沒有~？(= *Do you have any~?*)
lead〔lid〕*n.* 提示；線索
actually〔'æktʃuəlɪ〕*adv.* 事實上；實際上
rent〔rɛnt〕*n.* 出租　　*for rent* 出租的
building〔'bɪldɪŋ〕*n.* 建築物；大樓
across〔ə'krɔs〕*prep.* 在…的對面　　*thanks for⋯* 謝謝你⋯
tip〔tɪp〕*n.* 情報　　*check out* 檢查；看看
job〔dʒɑb〕*n.* 工作

22. (**C**) M : I'm not from around here. Could you point me in the
direction of the train station?
男：我不是這附近的人。你可以告訴我往火車站的方向嗎？
W : Sure. Just keep walking north until you reach the
city square. Stay to the right and you'll see the train
station.
女：當然。只要一直往北走，直到你抵達城市廣場。靠右邊走，
你就會看到火車站。
M : Thanks. I appreciate it.
男：謝謝。我很感激妳。
Question : Where does the man want to go?
男士要去哪裡？
(A) City Hall. 市政廳。
(B) The library. 圖書館。
(C) The train station. 火車站。

* point〔pɔɪnt〕*v.* 替⋯指路
direction〔də'rɛkʃən〕*n.* 方向；方位　　*train station* 火車站
keep + V-ing 持續~　　north〔nɔrθ〕*adv.* 向北
reach〔ritʃ〕*v.* 到達　　square〔skwɛr〕*n.* 廣場
stay〔ste〕*v.* 保持　　*to the right* 靠右邊
appreciate〔ə'priʃɪˌet〕*v.* 感激　　*city hall* 市政廳
library〔'laɪˌbrɛrɪ〕*n.* 圖書館

23. (**B**) W : I'd like to exchange this shirt. Do you have it in a
　　　　　　　smaller size?

　　　　女：我想要退換這件襯衫。你們有比較小的尺寸嗎？

　　　　M : Maybe. What size is the one you have?

　　　　男：可能有。妳那件是什麼尺寸？

　　　　W : It's a medium.

　　　　女：中號。

　　　　Question : What is wrong with the shirt?

　　　　　　　　襯衫有什麼問題？

　　　　(A) It's too expensive. 太貴了。

　　　　(B) It's too big. 太大了。

　　　　(C) It's the wrong color. 顏色不對。

　　　　* ***would like to V***. 想要～　　　exchange〔ɪksˈtʃendʒ〕*v.* 退換
　　　　shirt〔ʃɜt〕*n.* 襯衫　　size〔saɪz〕*n.* 尺寸
　　　　medium〔ˈmidɪəm〕*n.* 中號（M號）的衣服
　　　　What is wrong with…? …有什麼問題？
　　　　expensive〔ɪkˈspɛnsɪv〕*adj.* 昂貴的

24. (**C**) M : Have you lost weight, Maria? My goodness, you're
　　　　　　　as skinny as a fashion model!

　　　　男：妳瘦了嗎，瑪麗亞？天呀，妳跟時尚模特兒一樣皮包骨！

　　　　W : Actually, Norman, I have breast cancer. I've been
　　　　　　going through radiation therapy, which causes
　　　　　　patients to lose weight rapidly.

　　　　女：事實上，諾曼，我得了乳癌。我一直接受放射治療，這會讓
　　　　　　病人體重快速減少。

　　　　M : I'm so sorry, Maria. I had no idea. Please accept my
　　　　　　apology.

　　　　男：我很抱歉，瑪麗亞。我不知道。請接受我的道歉。

Question : What is wrong with Maria?

瑪麗亞怎麼了？

(A) She has an eating disorder. 她飲食失調。

(B) She has a brain tumor. 她有腦瘤。

(C) She has breast cancer. 她有乳癌。

* ***lose weight*** 減重   ***My goodness.*** 我的天啊。
skinny ('skɪnɪ) *adj.* 很瘦的；皮包骨的
fashion ('fæʃən) *n.* 時尚   model ('madḷ) *n.* 模特兒
breast (brɛst) *n.* 胸部；乳房   cancer ('kænsɚ) *n.* 癌症
go through 經歷；接受   radiation (,redɪ'eʃən) *n.* 放射線
therapy ('θɛrəpɪ) *n.* 治療法   cause (kɔz) *v.* 使
patient ('peʃənt) *n.* 病人   rapidly ('ræpɪdlɪ) *adv.* 快速地
have no idea 不知道   accept (ək'sɛpt) *v.* 接受
apology (ə'palədʒɪ) *n.* 道歉
disorder (dɪs'ɔrdɚ) *n.* 混亂；失調
eating disorder 飲食失調   brain (bren) *n.* 大腦
tumor ('tumɚ) *n.* 腫瘤

25. (**B**) W : I'm in the mood to see a movie tonight. What's in
the theaters these days?

女：我今晚想要看電影。最近電影院有什麼可以看？

M : You should probably ask my brother. He's the film
buff in the family.

男：妳應該問我弟弟。他是我家裡的電影迷。

W : Thanks. I'll do that.

女：謝謝。我會的。

Question : What does the man imply? 男士暗示什麼？

(A) He also wants to see a movie tonight.

他今晚也想去看電影。

(B) He doesn't pay much attention to movies.

他不太關注意電影。

(C) He is jealous of his brother's knowledge.

他羨慕他弟弟的知識。

* mood〔mud〕*n.* 心情　　***be in the mood to V.*** 想要～
theater〔ˈθiətə〕*n.* 電影院
these days 最近　　probably〔ˈprɑbəblɪ〕*adv.* 可能
film〔fɪlm〕*n.* 電影　　buff〔bʌf〕*n.* 愛好者；…迷
imply〔ɪmˈplaɪ〕*v.* 暗示
attention〔əˈtɛnʃən〕*n.* 注意（力）
pay attention to 注意
jealous〔ˈdʒɛləs〕*adj.* 羨慕的；嫉妒的＜*of*＞
knowledge〔ˈnɑlɪdʒ〕*n.* 知識

26. (**C**) M : That was a very entertaining story, Caroline. Thanks for letting me read it.

男：那是個很有趣的故事，卡羅琳。謝謝妳讓我讀這故事。

W : No, thank you for making the effort. I know it's a little longer than the average short story. I hope it didn't bore you.

女：不，謝謝你的努力。我知道這比一般的短篇小說長一點。我希望你不會覺得無聊。

M : Not at all. It was a pleasure from start to finish. You're an excellent writer.

男：一點也不。從頭到尾都讀得很愉快。妳是個優秀的作家。

Question : What did the woman write?

女士寫了什麼？

(A) A love letter. 一封情書。

(B) An epic poem. 一篇史詩。

(C) A short story. 一個短篇小說。

* entertaining〔͵ɛntə'tenɪŋ〕*adj.* 令人愉快的;有趣的
thanks for 謝謝你…   effort〔'ɛfət〕*n.* 努力
make an effort 努力;付出心血
average〔'ævərɪdʒ〕*adj.* 一般的   **short story** 短篇小說
bore〔bor〕*v.* 使厭倦;使無聊   **not at all** 一點也不
pleasure〔'plɛʒə〕*n.* 快樂的事
from start to finish 從開始到結束;自始至終
excellent〔'ɛkslənt〕*adj.* 優秀的
writer〔'raɪtə〕*n.* 作家   **love letter** 情書
epic〔'ɛpɪk〕*adj.* 史詩的   poem〔'po‧ɪm〕*n.* 詩

27. (**B**) W : The bus leaves at seven tomorrow morning, Tom.
　　　　　　Don't forget to set your alarm clock.

女:公車明天早上七點離開,湯姆。別忘了設鬧鐘。

M : Done. It's set for six-forty-five.

男:設好了。設定為六點四十五分。

W : Nice try, buddy. It takes you twenty minutes just to
　　get dressed. Set it for six-fifteen at the latest.

女:這樣是白費功夫,老弟。你穿衣服就要花二十分鐘。最晚要
　　設在六點十五分。

Question : What is the most probable relationship
　　　　　　between the woman and the man?

女士和男士最可能的關係是什麼?

(A) Teacher–student. 師生。

(B) Mother–son. 母子。

(C) Father–daughter. 父女。

* leave〔liv〕*v.* 離開   forget〔fə'gɛt〕*v.* 忘記
set〔sɛt〕*v.* 設定(鐘錶)   alarm〔ə'lɑrm〕*n.* 警報;鬧鐘

alarm clock 鬧鐘　　done〔dʌn〕*adj.* 完成的
nice try 【用於表示對方未達到目的】還不錯，但還不夠；
　白費功夫【詳見背景說明】
buddy〔'bʌdɪ〕*n.* 【用於稱呼】老兄；老弟
take〔tek〕*n.* 花費　　*get dressed* 穿衣服
probable〔'prɑbəbl〕*adj.* 可能的
relationship〔rɪ'leʃən‚ʃɪp〕*n.* 關係

28. (**B**) M : Do you know how long it takes for a letter to get
　　　　　　　　　from Taiwan to the U.S.?

男：妳知道一封信要多久時間才能從台灣到美國？

W : Five days if you send it via air mail. I'm not sure
　　　about the other options.

女：如果你寄航空郵件要五天。我不確定其他的方法要多久。

M : Hmm. Maybe I should consider using a next-day
　　delivery service.

男：嗯。或許我應該考慮用次日送達服務。

Question : What does the man imply? 男士暗示什麼？

(A) Air mail is too expensive. 航空郵件太貴。

(B) Air mail is not fast enough. 航空郵件不夠快。

(C) Air mail is the best option. 航空郵件是最好的選擇。

* take〔tek〕*v.* 花（時間）　　get〔gɛt〕*v.* 到達＜*to*＞
via〔'vaɪə〕*prep.* 透過；經由　　*air mail* 航空郵件
option〔'ɑpʃən〕*n.* 選擇
hmm〔hm〕*interj.* 【講話時停頓】嗯；唔
consider〔kən'sɪdɚ〕*v.* 考慮
delivery〔dɪ'lɪvərɪ〕*n.* 遞送　　service〔'sɝvɪs〕*n.* 服務
next-day delivery 次日遞送；次日送達
imply〔ɪm'plaɪ〕*v.* 暗示
expensive〔ɪks'pɛnsɪv〕*adj.* 昂貴的

29. (**B**) W : That's a nice watch. Is it real or a fake?

女：那是支好錶。那是眞的還是假的？

M : Thanks. I think it's a genuine Rolex. At least I hope
it is.

男：謝謝。我覺得這是貨眞價實的勞力士。至少我希望這支是。

W : You can usually tell by its weight.

女：你通常可以從它的重量來判斷。

Question : What are the speakers mainly discussing?

說話者主要在討論什麼？

(A) The woman's weight loss program. 女士的減重計畫。

(B) The man's watch. 男士的錶。

(C) The stranger's attitude. 陌生人的態度。

* fake〔fek〕*n.* 仿冒品　　genuine〔'dʒɛnjuɪn〕*adj.* 眞的
Rolex〔'rolɛks〕*n.* 勞力士錶　　*at least* 至少
usually〔'juʒʊəlɪ〕*adv.* 通常　　tell〔tɛl〕*v.* 判斷
mainly〔menlɪ〕*adv.* 主要地
discuss〔dɪ'skʌs〕*v.* 討論　　loss〔lɔs〕*n.* 減少
program〔'progræm〕*n.* 計畫
stranger〔'strendʒɚ〕*n.* 陌生人
attitude〔'ætə,tjud〕*n.* 態度

30. (**B**) M : What a beautiful day! Sunny skies, a light breeze
coming off the ocean…

男：眞是美好的一天！晴朗的天空，來自海洋輕柔的微風…

W : And what better place to spend it than at the beach?
No phone calls, no meetings, no deadlines. I feel so
relaxed.

女：要度過一天，有什麼更好的地方能比得上海灘？沒有電話、
不用開會、沒有截止期限。我覺得很放鬆。

M : We should do this more often. It's good to get out
of the office every once in a while.

男：我們應該更常這樣做。偶爾離開辦公室是很好的。

Question：What is implied about the speakers?

關於說話者，有什麼暗示？

(A) They have pale skin that burns easily.

他們皮膚很白，容易曬黑。

(B) They are taking a day off from work.

他們放了一天假。

(C) They will spend the next week at the beach.

他們下個禮拜會在海灘度過。

* beautiful〔'bjutəfəl〕*adj.* 美麗的；很棒的
sunny〔'sʌnɪ〕*adj.* 晴朗的　　sky〔skaɪ〕*n.* 天空
light〔laɪt〕*adj.* 輕的　　breeze〔briz〕*n.* 微風
ocean〔'oʃən〕*n.* 海洋
spend〔spɛnd〕*v.* 度過　　beach〔bitʃ〕*n.* 海灘
meeting〔'mitɪŋ〕*n.* 會議；開會
deadline〔'dɛd,laɪn〕*n.* 截止期限
relaxed〔rɪ'lækst〕*adj.* 放鬆的
get out of 離開；擺脫
office〔'ɔfɪs〕*n.* 辦公室
every once in a while 偶爾；有時候
pale〔pel〕*adj.* 蒼白的　　skin〔skɪn〕*n.* 皮膚
burn〔bɜn〕*v.* 曬黑　　***take a day off*** 放假一天

TEST 12

第一部分：辨識句意（第 1-10 題，共 10 題）

作答說明： 第 1-10 題每題均有三個選項，請依據所聽到的單句，選出符合描述的圖片。

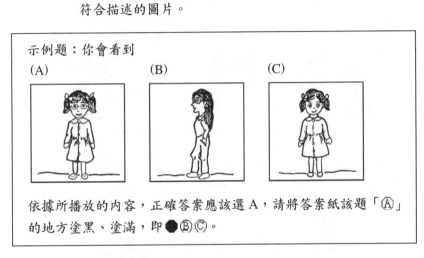

示例題：你會看到

(A)　　　　　(B)　　　　　(C)

依據所播放的內容，正確答案應該選 A，請將答案紙該題「Ⓐ」的地方塗黑、塗滿，即 ●ⒷⒸ。

1. (A)　　　　　(B)　　　　　(C)

2. (A)　　　　　(B)　　　　　(C)

3. (A)   (B)   (C)

4. (A)   (B)   (C)

5. (A)   (B)   (C)

6. (A)   (B)   (C)

7. (A)   (B)   (C)

8. (A)　　　　　　(B)　　　　　　(C)

9. (A)　　　　　　(B)　　　　　　(C)

10. (A)　　　　　　(B)　　　　　　(C)

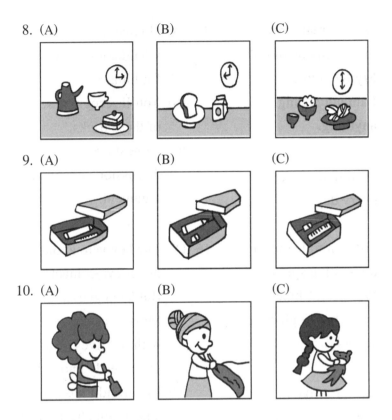

第二部分：基本問答（第 11-20 題，共 10 題）

作答説明： 第 11-20 題每題均有三個選項，請依據所聽到的對話問句，選出一個最適合的回答。

示例題：你會看到

(A) She is talking to the teacher.

(B) She is a student in my class.

(C) She is wearing a beautiful dress.

依據所播放的內容，正確答案應該選 B，請將答案紙該題「Ⓑ」的地方塗黑、塗滿，即Ⓐ●Ⓒ。

11. (A) Do you really need three pairs of shoes?
    (B) My feet hurt.
    (C) I am not selling anything.

12. (A) He did not write every day.
    (B) They are both difficult to learn for non-native speakers.
    (C) We speak Chinese at home but English in school.

13. (A) Sure, I'd like that.
    (B) You can say that again.
    (C) I can't believe it.

14. (A) It says, "No parking."
    (B) They say, "No smoking."
    (C) I said, "No fighting."

15. (A) No one in this town would consider voting for him.
    (B) You'll recognize some of these tricks.
    (C) Almost every discussion ends in an argument.

16. (A) The key is to avoid direct eye contact. But keep guessing.
    (B) Most of us are bored with our lives. But you already know that.
    (C) I'm afraid I have to take a rain check. But thanks for asking.

17. (A) Yes, I was thinking the same thing.
    (B) No, they were supposed to be here yesterday.
    (C) Sometimes I feel very scared.

18. (A) Thanks.
    (B) The Chicago Bears.
    (C) You're welcome.

19. (A) I didn't graduate.
    (B) It's not that kind of party.
    (C) She stood me up.

20. (A) The diner on Main Street is open until midnight.
    (B) The subway runs all night.
    (C) The waitress will bring the bill.

第三部分：言談理解（第 21-30 題，共 10 題）

作答說明：第 21-30 題每題均有三個選項，請依據所聽到的對話或短文內容，選出一個最適合的答案。

示例題：你會看到

(A) 9:50.　　(B) 10:00.　　(C) 10:10.

依據所播放的內容，正確答案應該選 B，請將答案紙該題「Ⓑ」的地方塗黑、塗滿，即 Ⓐ ● Ⓒ。

21. (A) In front.
    (B) In back.
    (C) On the side.

22. (A) Co-workers.
    (B) Classmates.
    (C) Neighbors.

23. (A) Soundly.
    (B) Loudly.
    (C) Poorly.

24. (A) Order a pizza.
    (B) Go to the market.
    (C) Make dinner.

25. (A) She enjoys mountain climbing.
    (B) She is an adventurous person.
    (C) She is afraid of high places.

26. (A) She is unemployed.
    (B) She is uneducated.
    (C) She is unemotional.

27. (A) In a classroom.
    (B) In an optometrist's office.
    (C) In an office building.

28. (A) Angry.
    (B) Uncomfortable.
    (C) Bored.

29. (A) In a fast-food restaurant.
    (B) In a fancy restaurant.
    (C) In a French restaurant.

30. (A) The woman is working very hard.
    (B) The woman should leave soon.
    (C) The woman doesn't like to fly.

TEST 12 詳解

第一部分：辨識句意

1. (**B**) (A)  (B) (C)

 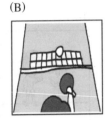 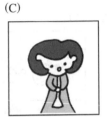

Nora is a good ping-pong player.
諾拉是很好的桌球選手。

   * ping-pong (ˈpɪŋˌpɑŋ) *n.* 乒乓球；桌球 (= *table tennis*)
   player (ˈpleɚ) *n.* 選手

2. (**B**) (A) (B) (C)

Let's have a barbeque. 我們來烤肉吧。

   * *let's* + *V.* 我們一起～吧   barbecue (ˈbɑrbɪˌkju) *n.* 烤肉

3. (**A**) (A) (B) (C)

The factory creates a lot of air pollution.

這間工廠製造許多的空氣污染。

* factory〔ˈfæktərɪ〕*n.* 工廠　　***a lot of*** 很多的
air〔ɛr〕*n.* 空氣　　pollution〔pəˈluʃən〕*n.* 污染

4. (**A**) (A)　　　　　　(B)　　　　　　(C)

Sam is as tall as the tree.　山姆跟樹一樣高。

* ***as…as~*** 和~一樣…　　　tall〔tl〕*adj.* 高的
tree〔tri〕*n.* 樹

5. (**A**) (A)　　　　　　(B)　　　　　　(C)

Jack is flying a kite.　傑克在放風箏。

* kite〔kaɪt〕*n.* 風箏　　***fly a kite*** 放風箏

6. (**A**) (A)　　　　　　(B)　　　　　　(C)

 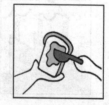

I'll have the fried eggs, please. 我要吃煎蛋，麻煩你。

* have〔hæv〕v. 吃；喝　　fried〔fraɪd〕adj. 油煎的

7. (**A**) (A)  (B)  (C)

Betty is decorating the Christmas tree. 貝蒂在佈置聖誕樹。

* decorate〔'dɛkə,ret〕v. 佈置；裝飾
　Christmas〔'krɪsməs〕adj. 聖誕節（用）的

8. (**C**) (A)  (B)  (C)

It's time for dinner. 現在該吃晚餐了。

* *it is time for* … 該是…的時候了　　dinner〔'dɪnə〕n. 晚餐

9. (**C**) (A)  (B) 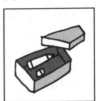 (C)

There's a ruler and an eraser in the box.
盒子裡有一支尺和一個橡皮擦。

* ruler〔'rulə〕n. 尺　　eraser〔ɪ'resə〕n. 橡皮擦

10. (**A**) (A)  (B)  (C)

Mom is a good cook.　我媽媽是個好廚師。

* cook〔kʊk〕*n.* 廚師

二、基本問答

11. (**A**) Look, these shoes are on sale.　Buy two pairs, get one free.　你看，這些鞋子在特價。買兩雙，第三雙免費。

(A) Do you really need three pairs of shoes?

你真的需要三雙鞋嗎？

(B) My feet hurt.　我的腳很痛。

(C) I am not selling anything.

我不是在賣東西的。

* look〔lʊk〕*v.* 看；瞧　　***on sale***　特價中
pair〔pɛr〕*n.* 一對；一雙　　free〔fri〕*adj.* 免費的
feet〔fit〕*n. pl.* 雙腳【單數是 foot】　　hurt〔hɝt〕*v.* 疼痛
sell〔sɛl〕*v.* 賣

12. (**B**) Which language is harder to learn, Chinese or English?

哪一種語言比較難學，中文還是英文？

(A) He did not write every day.　他沒有每天寫。

(B) They are both difficult to learn for non-native speakers.　對非母語者來說都很難。

(C) We speak Chinese at home but English in school.

我們在家說中文，但在學校說英文。

* language〔'læŋgwɪdʒ〕*n.* 語言　learn〔lɜn〕*v.* 學
write〔wraɪt〕*v.* 寫（字）；寫作
non-〔nɑn〕（字首）表示「非…」
native〔'netɪv〕*adj.* 本國的；本土的
native speaker 講母語的人

13. (**A**) We're going to see a movie.　Want to come?
我們要去看電影。要來嗎？

　　(A) Sure, I'd like that. 當然，我想去。

　　(B) You can say that again. 我非常同意。

　　(C) I can't believe it. 我無法相信。

　　* sure〔ʃʊr〕*adv.* 當然
　　would like 想要　***You can say that again.*** 我非常同意。
　　believe〔bə'liv〕*v.* 相信

14. (**A**) I don't have my glasses with me.　Can you read what the
sign says for me?
我沒有把眼鏡帶在身上。你可以告訴我告示牌上說什麼嗎？

　　(A) It says, "No parking." 它說：「禁止停車。」

　　(B) They say, "No smoking." 他們說：「禁止抽煙。」

　　(C) I said, "No fighting." 我說：「不可以打架。」

　　* glasses〔'glæsɪz〕*n. pl.* 眼鏡
　　sign〔saɪn〕*n.* 標誌；告示牌　　park〔pɑrk〕*v.* 停車
　　smoke〔smok〕*v.* 抽煙　　fight〔faɪt〕*v.* 打架

15. (**A**) I can't believe Tom Smith is running for mayor.
我無法相信湯姆・史密斯要競選鎮長。

　　(A) No one in this town would consider voting for him.
　　　沒有一個鎮民會考慮投票給他。

　　(B) You'll recognize some of these tricks.
　　　你會發現一些騙人的伎倆。

(C) Almost every discussion ends in an argument.
幾乎每次討論都是以爭執收場。

* run〔 rʌn 〕v. 競選＜*for*＞　　mayor〔'meɚ〕n. 市長；鎮長
  consider〔 kən'sɪdɚ〕v. 考慮
  vote〔 vot 〕v. 投票　　***vote for*** 投票給
  recognize〔'rɛkəg,naɪz〕v. 認出；看出
  trick〔 trɪk 〕n. 詭計；騙人的伎倆
  discussion〔 dɪ'skʌʃən〕n. 討論　　***end in*** 以…作爲結束
  argument〔'ɑrgjəmənt〕n. 爭論

16. (**C**) We're going to Murphy's for a drink.　Care to join us?
我們要去莫非酒吧喝一杯。想要加入我們嗎？

  (A) The key is to avoid direct eye contact.　But keep
guessing. 重點是要避免直接的目光接觸。但是要繼續猜測。

  (B) Most of us are bored with our lives.　But you already
know that.
我們大多數的人都覺得生活無聊。但是你已經知道這件事了。

  (C) I'm afraid I have to take a rain check.　But thanks for
asking. 我恐怕得改天了。不過還是謝謝你的邀請。

* drink〔 drɪŋk 〕n. 飲料；（酒）一杯　　***care to*** V. 想要~
  join〔 dʒɔɪn 〕v. 加入　　key〔 ki 〕n. 關鍵；重點
  avoid〔 ə'vɔɪd 〕v. 避免　　direct〔 də'rɛkt 〕adj. 直接的
  contact〔'kɑntækt〕n. 接觸　　***eye contact*** 目光接觸
  guess〔 gɛs 〕v. 猜測　　***be bored with*** 厭倦
  I am afraid… 我恐怕…　　***rain check*** 延期；改期
  Thanks for asking. 謝謝你的邀請。

17. (**A**) Ted is leaving tomorrow.　We should take him out for his
last night in town.
泰德明天就要離開了。我們應該邀他出來度過在鎮上的最後一晚。

  (A) Yes, I was thinking the same thing.
是的，我也是這樣想。

(B) No, they were supposed to be here yesterday.
不，他們應該昨天就到這裡。

(C) Sometimes I feel very scared. 有時候我覺得很害怕。

* *take sb. out* 邀請某人外出　　*be supposed to V.* 應該～
sometimes〔'sʌm,taɪmz〕*adv.* 有時候；偶爾
scared〔skɛrd〕*adj.* 害怕的

18. (**A**) That was a great game, Terrance. You played very well.
那是場很棒的比賽，泰瑞斯。你打得很好。

(A) Thanks. 謝謝。

(B) The Chicago Bears. 芝加哥熊隊。

(C) You're welcome. 不客氣。

* play〔ple〕*v.* 參加比賽
The Chicago Bear 芝加哥熊隊【美國的一支橄欖球隊】
You're welcome. 不客氣。

19. (**C**) What are you doing home, Mike? I thought you had a date. 你在家做什麼，麥克？我以為你有約會。

(A) I didn't graduate. 我沒有畢業。

(B) It's not that kind of party. 不是那種派對。

(C) She stood me up. 她放我鴿子。

* date〔det〕*n.* 約會　　graduate〔'grædʒʊ,et〕*v.* 畢業
stand sb. up 放某人鴿子

20. (**A**) Look at the time. We should grab a bite to eat before it gets too late.
看一下時間。在還沒太晚之前，我們應該隨便吃個東西。

(A) The diner on Main Street is open until midnight.
主街的小餐館開到半夜。

(B) The subway runs all night. 地下鐵整晚都有開。

(C) The waitress will bring the bill.
女服務生會把帳單拿過來。

* grab〔græb〕*v.* 抓；急著用　　bite〔baɪt〕*n.* 咬；一小口食物
grab a bite 簡單吃點東西　　diner〔'daɪnə〕*n.* 小餐館
main〔men〕*adj.* 主要的　　midnight〔'mɪd,naɪt〕*n.* 半夜
subway〔'sʌb,we〕*n.* 地下鐵　　run〔rʌn〕*v.* 通行；行駛
waitress〔'wetrɪs〕*n.* 女服務生　　bill〔bɪl〕*n.* 帳單

第三部分：言談理解

21. (**A**)　W：The seminar is about to begin.　Let's get a seat up
front.
女：研討會要開始了。我們來坐前面的位子。

M：I'd rather sit in the back, if you don't mind.　I might
have to leave early.
男：我寧願坐在後面，如果妳不介意的話。我可能得提早走。

W：OK, do as you please.　I'll see you later.
女：好吧，隨便你。我晚點再跟你見面。

Question：Where does the woman want to sit?
　　　　　女士想坐在哪裡？

(A) In front.　在前面。

(B) In back.　在後面。

(C) On the side.　在側面。

* seminar〔'sɛmə,nɑr〕*n.* 研討會　　**be about to V.** 即將～
seat〔sit〕*n.* 座位　　up〔ʌp〕*adv.* 向前
front〔frʌnt〕*adv.* 在前面　　**would rather** 寧願
mind〔maɪnd〕*v.* 介意　　please〔pliz〕*v.* 高興；喜歡
do as you please 隨你的意思去做
side〔saɪd〕*n.* 旁邊；側邊

22. (**A**)　M：Let me know when you're done with the marketing
report, Jenny.
男：當妳做完行銷報告時跟我說，珍妮。

W：Will do, Harry.　Give me another hour or so.
女：我會的，哈利。再給我一小時左右。

M : Great! I'll be in my office.

男：很好！我會在辦公室裡。

Question : What is the most likely relationship between the speakers? 說話者最可能的關係是什麼？

(A) Co-workers. 同事。

(B) Classmates. 同班同學。

(C) Neighbors. 鄰居。

* ***be done with*** 結束；完成
  marketing〔'mɑrkɪtɪŋ〕*n.* 行銷　***…or so*** 大約…
  office〔'ɔfɪs〕*n.* 辦公室　likely〔'laɪklɪ〕*adj.* 可能的
  relationship〔rɪ'leʃən‚ʃɪp〕*n.* 關係
  co-worker〔'ko'wɜkɚ〕*n.* 同事
  neighbor〔'nebɚ〕*n.* 鄰居

23. (**C**) W : Good morning, Brad. How did you sleep?

女：早安，布萊德。你睡得如何？

M : I tossed and turned the whole night.

男：我整晚輾轉難眠。

W : I'm sorry to hear that. Was it something to do with the bed?

女：很遺憾聽到這樣的事。這跟床有關嗎？

Question : How did Brad sleep last night?

昨晚布萊德睡得如何？

(A) Soundly. 很熟。

(B) Loudly. 很大聲。

(C) Poorly. 很差。

* toss〔tɔs〕*v.* 輾轉反側　turn〔tɜn〕*v.* 翻轉
  toss and turn 翻來覆去；輾轉難眠
  whole〔hol〕*adj.* 整個的　sorry〔'sɔrɪ〕*adj.* 遺憾的
  soundly〔'saʊndlɪ〕*adv.* (睡得) 很熟地
  poorly〔'pʊrlɪ〕*adv.* 很差地；不足地

24. (**A**) M : I'm going to order a pizza from Domino's. Any
preferences?

男：我要訂達美樂披薩。有偏好的口味嗎？

W : No onions or bell peppers.

女：不要洋蔥或甜椒。

M : OK, no problem. How about pepperoni?

男：好的，沒問題。那義大利臘味香腸如何。

Question : What is the man going to do?

男士要做什麼？

(A) Order a pizza. 訂披薩。

(B) Go to the market. 去市場。

(C) Make dinner. 做晚餐。

* order〔'ɔrfɚ〕*v.* 訂購　　pizza〔'pitsə〕*n.* 披薩
Domino's 達美樂披薩【連鎖披薩店】
preference〔'prɛfərəns〕*n.* 偏好
onion〔'ʌnjən〕*n.* 洋蔥　　***bell pepper*** 甜椒
How about~? ～如何？
pepperoni〔ˌpɛpə'ronɪ〕*n.* 義大利臘味香腸
market〔'mɑrkɪt〕*n.* 市場

25. (**C**) M : What's the highest mountain you've ever climbed?

男：妳爬過最高的山是哪座？

W : Me? I don't climb anything. I'm terrified of heights.

女：我？我什麼都不爬。我怕高。

M : Really? I thought you were the adventurous
type.

男：真的嗎？我以為妳是愛冒險的那種人。

Question : What is true about the woman?

關於女士何者為真？

(A) She enjoys mountain climbing. 她喜愛爬山。

(B) She is an adventurous person. 她是個愛冒險的人。

(C) She is afraid of high places. 她害怕高的地方。

* climb〔klaɪm〕v. 爬；攀登
terrified〔'tɛrə,faɪd〕adj. 害怕的 < of >
heights〔haɪts〕n. pl. 高處；高地
consider〔kən'sɪdɚ〕v. 認為
adventurous〔əd'vɛntʃərəs〕n. 愛冒險的
type〔taɪp〕n. …類型的人
enjoy〔ɪn'dʒɔɪ〕v. 喜愛
mountain climbing 爬山　　***be afraid of*** 害怕

26. (**A**) M : I read in the newspaper this morning that they're
accepting applications at Wal-mart, Helen.

男：我今天早上在報紙上看到他們在沃爾瑪超市接收應徵，海倫。

W : What are you trying to say, Bob? Are you implying
that I need to get a job?

女：你想要說什麼，鮑伯？你在暗示我需要找份工作嗎？

M : No, I was just passing on the information. There was
no hidden meaning in what I said.

男：不，我只是在傳達訊息。我話裡沒有什麼言外之意。

Question : What do we know about Helen?

關於海倫我們知道什麼？

(A) She is unemployed. 她沒有工作。

(B) She is uneducated. 她未受教育。

(C) She is unemotional. 她很冷靜。

* accept〔ək'sɛpt〕v. 接受
application〔,æplə'keʃən〕n. 申請；應徵
Wal-mart 沃爾瑪超市【連鎖超市】
imply〔ɪm'plaɪ〕v. 暗示　　***get a job*** 找工作
pass on 傳遞
information〔,ɪnfɚ'meʃən〕n. 資訊；消息

hidden〔'hɪdn̩〕*adj.* 隱藏的　　meaning〔'minɪŋ〕*n.* 意義
hidden meaning 言外之意
unemployed〔͵ʌnɪm'plɔɪd〕*adj.* 失業的；沒有工作的
uneducated〔ʌn'ɛdʒʊ͵ketɪd〕*adj.* 未受教育的
unemotional〔͵ʌnɪ'moʃən̩l〕*adj.* 不動感情的；冷靜的

27. (**C**)　W：I found a couple of typos in the sales report. You
　　　　　　　　might want to correct them before you pass it on to
　　　　　　　　Mr. Emerson.

　　女：我發現銷售報告裡有幾個打字的錯誤。你可能要在交給愛
　　　　默生先生之前改正那些錯誤。

　　M：Thanks, Rita. Did anything else jump out at you?

　　男：謝謝，瑞塔。妳有注意到什麼其他的事嗎？

　　W：Emerson has bad eyesight, so I'd probably use a
　　　　larger font. But overall, it's pretty solid.

　　女：愛默生視力不好，所以我可能會用大一點的字體。但整體
　　　　來說，這很完整。

　　Question：Where did this conversation probably take
　　　　　　　　place? 這對話可能是在哪裡發生的？

　(A) In a classroom. 在教室。

　(B) In an optometrist's office. 在驗光師的辦公室。

　(C) In an office building. 在辦公大樓。

* ***a couple of*** 幾個　　typo〔'taɪpo〕*n.* 打字錯誤
sales〔selz〕*adj.* 銷售的　　report〔rɪ'port〕*n.* 報告
correct〔kə'rɛkt〕*v.* 改正
jump out at sb. 引起某人注意（ = *be noticeable to sb.* ）
eyesight〔'aɪ͵saɪt〕*n.* 視力　　probably〔'prɑbəblɪ〕*adv.* 可能
font〔fɑnt〕*n.* 字型；字體　　overall〔'ovɚ͵ɔl〕*adv.* 整體來說
pretty〔'prɪtɪ〕*adv.* 相當；非常
solid〔'sɑlɪd〕*adj.* 充實的；完整的
optometrist〔ɑp'tɑmətrɪst〕*n.* 驗光師
office building 辦公大樓

28. (**B**)　W：I'm running late, Jim. Why don't you go and I'll catch up with you later?

女：我要遲到了，吉姆。你何不先走，我等會再追上你？

M：I'm not in any rush, Evelyn. Take your time.

男：我不急，伊芙琳。慢慢來。

W：Well, the thing is, I'm not comfortable with making you wait. Please, just go.

女：嗯，重點是，讓你等我覺得不自在。請你就先走吧。

Question：How does the woman feel?

女士覺得如何？

(A) Angry. 生氣的。

(B) Uncomfortable. 不自在的。

(C) Bored. 無聊的。

* ***be running late*** 快遲到了
　Why don't you ~? 你何不 ~ ？
　catch up with 趕上；追上　　rush〔 rʌʃ 〕*n.* 匆忙
　be in a rush 急急忙忙；匆忙　　***take one's time*** 慢慢來
　the thing is… 問題是…；重要的是…
　comfortable〔ˈkʌmfɚtəbļ〕*adj.* 舒服的；自在的
　uncomfortable〔 ʌnˈkʌmfɚtəbļ〕*adj.* 不舒服的；不自在的
　bored〔 bord 〕*adj.* 無聊的

29. (**A**)　M：Your total is seven sixty-four. Is that for here or to go?

男：妳的總共是 7.64 元。內用還是外帶？

W：To go. Can I pay for this with my debit card?

女：外帶。可以用簽帳卡付款嗎？

M：Sorry, ma'am. Cash only.

男：抱歉，小姐。只收現金。

Question：Where is this conversation probably taking place? 這對話最可能出現在哪裡？

(A) In a fast-food restaurant. 速食餐廳裡。

(B) In a fancy restaurant. 高級餐廳裡。

(C) In a French restaurant. 法國餐廳裡。

* total〔ˈtotl̩〕*n.* 總額　　***for here*** 內用
to go 外帶　　pay〔pe〕*v.* 付款 <*for*>
debit〔ˈdɛbɪt〕*n.* 提取的款項　　***debit card*** 簽帳卡
ma'am〔mæm〕*n.* 小姐；太太（= *madam*）
cash〔kæʃ〕*n.* 現金　　***Cash only.*** 只收現金。
fast-food〔ˈfæstˌfud〕*adj.* 速食的
restaurant〔ˈrɛstərənt〕*n.* 餐廳
fancy〔ˈfænsɪ〕*adj.* 昂貴的；高級的
French〔frɛntʃ〕*adj.* 法國的

30. (**B**) M：Your flight is at 5:30. What time are you leaving for the airport?

男：妳的班機是五點三十分。妳幾點要前往機場？

W：I've still got time. I like to be the last one on the plane.

女：我還有時間。我想要最後一個上飛機。

M：Aren't you cutting it a bit close? It's 3:30 now.

男：妳不會要把時間掐得這麼緊吧？現在三點三十分了。

Question：What does the man imply? 男士暗示什麼？

(A) The woman is working very hard. 女士正努力工作。

(B) The woman should leave soon. 女士應該儘快出發。

(C) The woman doesn't like to fly. 女士不喜歡搭飛機。

* flight〔flaɪt〕*n.* 班機　　***leave for*** 動身前往
airport〔ˈɛrˌport〕*n.* 機場　　***have got*** 有（= *have*）
plane〔plen〕*n.* 飛機　　***a bit*** 稍微；有點
cut it close 時間掐得緊（= *cut it fine*）
work〔wɝk〕*v.* 工作　　hard〔hard〕*adv.* 努力地
fly〔flaɪ〕*v.* 搭飛機

● 背景說明

本書有許多美國人常用的口語，非常生活化且實用，特地總結在這裡說明，以供參考。(回-頁數-題)

1. *He'll be in line*. (1-11-13)

in line 有「排隊等候」的意思，所以這句話字面的意思是「他會排隊等候。」引申為「他會是得到⋯的人」，後面常接 for。例如：Who is *in line for* a promotion? (誰有可能獲得升遷？)

> *be in line for* 有可能獲得 (= *be likely to receive*)
> promotion〔 prə'moʃən 〕*n.* 升遷

2. *I take it without*. (1-18-26)

這句話依據上下文可以寫成：I take it without cream or sugar. (我咖啡不加奶精或糖。) 這裡的 take 是「吃；喝」(= *eat*; *drink*)；因為上一句已經有 cream or sugar，所以這句的回答就省略了。類似的用法：*do without* (沒有⋯而將就一下)，例如：I can't afford to buy her new sneakers, so I'm afraid she will just have to *do without*. (我沒錢買給她新的運動鞋，恐怕她得將就一下了。)

> afford〔 ə'ford 〕*v.* 買得起
> sneakers〔'snikəz 〕*n. pl.* 運動鞋

3. *I can't complain*. (2-10-11)

這句話字面意思是「我無法抱怨。」換句話說，沒事情好抱怨就是「我感到很滿意。」是一種用否定的方式來表示肯定的說法，也可以說成：

I can't complain.

= Nothing to complain about.

= Things are going very well.

【go〔go〕*v.* 進行】

4. *Could I catch a ride downtown with you tomorrow morning, Rita?* (2-15-22)

這句話的意思是「瑞塔，我明天早上可以搭妳的車到市中心嗎？」catch a ride with *sb*.是「搭某人的便車」：

{
catch a ride with sb.
= hitch a ride with *sb*.
= hitch a lift with *sb*.
}

{
= get a ride with *sb*.
= ride with *sb*.
}

hitch〔hɪtʃ〕*v.* 搭（便車）　　lift〔lɪft〕*n.* 乘車

5. *Another cup might put me over the edge*. (2-19-28)

這句話字面的意思是「再喝一杯可能會讓我超出邊緣。」over the edge 引申為「超出負荷；使無法忍受」的意思。

put one over the edge
= *one* has reached *one's* limit
= *one* can't take anymore

reach〔ritʃ〕*v.* 達到
limit〔'lɪmɪt〕*n.* 極限
take〔tek〕*v.* 忍受

6. *Make it more like eight years, Dick.* (3-11-13)

　　這句話的意思是「我覺得好像有八年了，狄克。」這裡的 make 是「認為；估計」的意思；it 是代替「時間」；這裡的主詞 I 省略了。類似的用法有：What time do you make it? (你覺得現在幾點？)

Make it more like eight years, Dick.
= In fact, it is more like eight years.

【*in fact* 事實上】

7. *She doesn't look a day over 40.* (4-16-25)

　　這句話字面意思是「她看起來不超過四十歲一天。」也就是「她看起來不到四十歲」的意思。年齡也可以換成五十歲、六十歲等。

She doesn't look a day over 40.
= She looks younger than 40.
= She looks on the right side of 40.

【*on the right side of* 未滿…歲】

8. *Just a bit of sugar; hold the cream.* (7-11-13)

　　這句話字面意思是「一點糖，保留奶精。」意思就是「加糖，不加奶精」。這是常見的美式口語，例如：Give me a hot dog, but hold the mustard. (給我熱狗，不要芥末。) 其他說法像是：hold the chili (不要加辣椒)【詳見「麥克米倫高級英漢雙解辭典」p.954】

> *Just a bit of sugar; hold the cream.*
> = Just a bit of sugar; spare the cream.
> = Just a bit of sugar; skip the cream.
> = Just a bit of sugar; leave out the cream.

> = Just a bit of sugar, without the cream.
> = Just a bit of sugar, minus the cream.
> = Just a bit of sugar, sans the cream.

mustard〔'mʌstəd〕*n.* 芥末
chili〔'tʃɪlɪ〕*n.* 辣椒　　spare〔spɛr〕*v.* 不用；省下
skip〔skɪp〕*v.* 跳過；省去　　*leave out* 省去
minus〔'maɪnəs〕*prep.* 減去；沒有…的
sans〔sænz〕*prep.* 沒有；缺…

9. *Tomorrow never knows*. (10-11-13)

這句諺語字面的意思是「明天永遠不會知道。」意思
就是「無人能預知明天；世事難料。」

Tomorrow never knows.
= Who knows what tomorrow may bring.
= The future is uncertain.
= Live for today.

uncertain〔ʌn'sɝtn̩〕*adj.* 不確定的
Live for today. 【諺】爲今日而活；活在當下。

10. *You could see it coming a mile away*. (10-13-17)

這句話字面意思是「你可以看到它從一哩的地方走過
來。」這裡的 it，指的是問題裡面的 the ending（結局），

see *sth.* come a mile away，意思是「從一哩的地方看到某件事」，引申為「知道某事即將發生」(= *notice that something is going to happen*)。

> ***You could see it coming a mile away.***
> = It was obvious.
> = It was hardly surprising.
>
> > obvious (ˈɑbvɪəs) *adj.* 明顯的
> > hardly (ˈhɑrdlɪ) *adv.* 幾乎不
> > surprising (səˈpraɪzɪŋ) *adj.* 令人驚訝的

11. *The money just isn't there*. (10-13-17)

這句話字面的意思是「錢就不在那裡。」引申為「沒有錢；付不起。」

> ***The money just isn't there.***
> = We don't have the money.
> = We can't afford it.
>
> 【afford (əˈford) *v.* 負擔得起】

12. *I didn't know you had it in you*. (10-14-20)

這句話字面的意思是「我不知道你有這個東西。」意思就是「我不知道你做得到；我不到你有這個能耐。」have it in *one* 是「有能力（或勇氣）」的意思。這裡的 it，通常要靠上下文來決定。例如：He doesn't have it in him to cheat. (他做不了騙人的事。) it 就是指後面的不定詞 to cheat (欺騙)。

另一個說法是：have what it takes (to V.)，字面的意思是「有去（做…）的能力」，也就是「有能力（做…）」的意思，例如：Do you think Ken's got what it takes to be a doctor? (你覺得肯能成為好醫生嗎？)

I didn't know you had it in you.
= I didn't know you were capable of it.

capable〔'kepəbḷ〕*adj.* 有能力的
be capable of 能做得出…的

13. *Nice try, buddy.* (11-20-27)

這句話字面的意思是「很好的嘗試，老弟。」這裡的 Nice try 是反諷的語氣，表示「很不錯，但是你沒有真的做到；白費功夫」。要靠上下文來理解，也可以說成 Good try，例如：Good try, but do you really think I would believe that? (你騙不了我的，你真的以為我會相信嗎？)
或是：Nice try. I wasn't born yesterday, you know.
(想騙我。我可不是三歲小孩。)

Nice try.
= Good try.
= You didn't fool me.

【fool〔ful〕*v.* 愚弄；欺騙】